THE THIRTY-SIX DRAMATIC SITUATIONS

"Gozzi maintained that there can be but thirty-six tragic situations. Schiller took great pains to find more, but he was unable to find even so many as Gozzi."—Goethe.

The
Thirty-Six Dramatic
Situations

GEORGES POLTI
Translated by Lucille Ray

Boston
THE WRITER, INC.
Publishers

Reprinted   1984

Library of Congress Cataloging in Publication Data

Polti, Georges, 1868–
  The thirty-six dramatic situations.

  Translation of Les trente-six situations dramatiques.
  1. Plots (Drama, novel, etc.) 2. Drama—Technique.
I. Ray, Lucille.   II. Title.
PN218.P6413   1977   808.8'024   77-8343
ISBN 0-87116-109-5

Manufactured in the United States of America

THE THIRTY-SIX DRAMATIC SITUATIONS

PREFACE

Where do plots come from? Are there actually any original plots for fiction or drama? These are questions frequently asked by novelists, dramatists, and short story writers, who are often told that there are no new plots, but rather that authors spin their plots from a relatively small number of "basic situations," changing characters, reversing roles, giving modern twists to classic themes.

In *The Thirty-Six Dramatic Situations,* Georges Polti shows that all possible plots are variations of only thirty-six basic plots, and his original analysis identifies and defines these fundamental human emotional conflicts, on which all literary works are based.

Using examples from literature, Polti tells how some of the best-known and best-loved novels, stories, and plays have been developed from these basic situations, and how writers draw on them as an almost limitless source of plot ideas. Each of the "situations" cited by Polti suggests a new approach, building on fresh insights into human actions and interactions. These classifications provide a springboard for "original" plotting directions, in which authors add their imagination, skill, and inventiveness to Polti's insights into human behavior.

A few examples from *The Thirty-Six Dramatic Situations* will illustrate how successfully Polti's delineation of "basic" plots can be made to serve a fiction writer or dramatist. The Sixth Situation is "Disaster," in which one section deals with "natural disaster." This covers many classic works, for example, H. G. Wells's novel *The War of the Worlds,* in which elements of the story include "A vanquished power; a victorious enemy; fear, catastrophe, the unforeseen, a great reversal of roles; the powerful are overthrown, the weak exalted. . . ." Other examples include Shakespeare's *Richard II* and *King Lear.* In modern novels, plots based on "Disaster" include a major success like Richard Martin Stern's *The Tower,* the novel about a skyscraper fire which, in combination with another novel about a similar fire — *The Glass Inferno,* by Thomas N. Scortia and Frank M. Robinson — was made into a popular motion picture, *The Towering Inferno.* Changes in the cause of the disaster, a completely contemporary setting with the characters that are appropriate to it, transform the "disaster" theme into a satisfying plot for today's audiences. And Clive Cussler's best-selling *Raise the Titanic* is another present-day example of a novel based on the "Disaster" situation, in modern and future times, with political overtones.

Gone with the Wind, by Margaret Mitchell, uses two situations joined together to make the plot: "Daring Enterprises" (the Ninth Situation) and "Obstacles to Love" (the Twenty-Eighth Situation). Many modern adventure stories and novels are variations of "Daring Enterprises." In some the motivation is evil, as in the case of *The Day of the Jackal* by Frederick Forsyth. Exploration of distant planets inhabited by dangerous creatures, the substance of so many science fiction tales and television plays, also falls within this category — a good illustration of taking a basic situation into places unknown, adding some scientific background, and imaginative characters invented by the writer.

The Twenty-first Situation — "Self-Sacrifice for Kindred" — is found in a wide range of plays, stories, and novels: *Measure for Measure* by Shakespeare, Rostand's *Cyrano de Bergerac, Great Expectations* by Dickens,

Ethan Frome by Edith Wharton (in which the motivation is not love, but guilt and duty).

In Shakespeare's *Romeo and Juliet,* as well as in Somerset Maugham's famous story, "Miss Thompson" (which was made into the play and motion picture *Rain*), we have memorable but widely different examples of the Twenty-Second Situation — "All Sacrificed for a Passion."

Literary examples of "Crime Pursued by Vengeance" (the Third Situation) exist in *The Count of Monte Cristo* (Dumas), *Les Miserables* (Victor Hugo), Shakespeare's *The Merchant of Venice,* the Sherlock Holmes stories, and more recently, in the mystery novels of Georges Simenon, Agatha Christie (*Murder on the Orient Express*), Ross Macdonald, and others, with countless variations, depending upon the setting, motivation, and characters.

To illustrate the "Remorse" plot (the Thirty-Fourth Situation), Polti suggests Dostoevsky's *Crime and Punishment.* The legend of Pandora and the tale of Bluebeard are vivid examples of plots based on "Fatal Imprudence," or curiosity (the Seventeenth Situation); and innumerable plots hinge on the foolish — or brave — characters who have ventured into locked rooms only to find untold horrors, who go out of safe harbors into predictably hazardous waters, and who have generally disobeyed orders against exploring the fearful and unknown.

The various sub-classifications in Polti's *Thirty-Six Dramatic Situations* offer fiction writers and playwrights an unending source of plot ideas, which can combine in plot patterns they may never before have considered. Polti's classifications and categories are based on universal emotions, as valid now as they were in ancient times when storytelling took place around campfires and in primitive villages; these human situations and emotions may be applied to the people and events of life in every generation — their use is limited only by the imagination of the writer. Like a kaleidoscope, these "dramatic situations" can be made into new and relevant plots for today's readers by changing one or more of the facets or elements. *The Thirty-Six Dramatic Situations* remains as valuable and stimulating a source of plots as it was when Georges Polti first wrote it, and it continues to spark the imagination and inventiveness of writers everywhere.

INTRODUCTION

"Gozzi maintained that there can be but thirty-six tragic situations. Schiller took great pains to find more, but he was unable to find even so many as Gozzi."

Thirty-six situations only! There is, to me, something tantalizing about the assertion, unaccompanied as it is by any explanation either from Gozzi, or from Goethe or Schiller, and presenting a problem which it does not solve. For I remembered that he who declared by this limited number so strongly synthetic a law, had himself the most fantastic of imaginations. He was the author, this Gozzi, of "Turandot," and of the "Roi Cerf," two works almost without analogue, the one upon the situation of the "Enigma," the other upon phases of metempsychosis; he was the creator of a dramatic system, and the Arabesque spirit, through him transfused, has given us the work of Hoffmann, Jean-Paul Richter and Poe.

The Venetian's exuberance would have made me doubtful of him, since, having once launched at us this number 36, he kept silence. But Schiller, rigid and ardent Kantian, prince of modern aestheticians, master of true historic drama,—had he not in turn, before accepting this rule, "taken great pains" to verify it (and the pains of a Schiller!) thereby giving it the additional authority of his powerful criticism and his rich memory? And Goethe, his opposite in all things save a strong taste for the abstract,—Goethe, who throughout his life seems to have considered the subject, adds his testimony years after the death of Schiller, years after their fruitful conversations, at the very time when he was completing "Faust," that supreme combination of contrasting elements.

In France, Gérard de Nerval alone had grasped and presented briefly the ensemble of all dramatic production, in an article upon Soumet's "Jane Grey," in "L'Artiste,"—written, unfortunately, with what dandyism of style! Having early desired to know the exact number of actions possible to the theatre, he found, he tells us, twenty-four. His basis, however, is far from satisfactory. Falling back upon the outworn classification of the seven capital sins, he finds himself obliged at the outset to eliminate two of them, gluttony and sloth, and very nearly a third, lust (this would be Don Juan, perhaps). It is not apparent what manner of tragic energy has ever been furnished by avarice, and the divergence between pride (presumably the spirit of tyranny) and danger, does not promise well for the contexture of drama, the manifestations of the latter being too easily confounded with those of envy. Furthermore, murder or homicide, which he indicates as a factor for obtaining several new situations, by uniting it in turn with each of the others, cannot be accepted as such, since it is but an accident common to all of them, possible in all, and one most frequently produced by all. And finally, the sole title mentioned by Nerval, "Rivalry of Queen and Subject," corresponds, it will be observed, only to a sub-class of one, not of his twenty-four, but of Gozzi's Thirty-six Situations.

Since Nerval, no one has treated, in Gozzi's genuinely technical manner, of the secrets of invention, unless it be relevant to mention in this connection Sarcey's celebrated theory of the "scène-à-faire," a theory in general but ill comprehended by an age which dreads didacticism,—that is to say, dreads any serious reflection upon art; some intimate notes of Dumas *fils* which were published against his wishes, if my youthful memories are correct, in the "Temps" some years ago, and which set forth that double plot of Corneille and Racine, a heroine disputed by two heroes, and a hero disputed by two heroines; and, lastly, some works here and there by Valin, upon composition. And that is all, absolutely all.

Finally, in brief, I rediscovered the thirty-six situations, as Gozzi doubtless possessed them, and as the reader will find them in the following pages; for there were indeed, as he had indicated, thirty-six categories which I had to formulate in order to distribute fitly among them the innumerable dramas awaiting classification. There is, I hasten to say, nothing mystic or cabalistic about this particular number; it might perhaps be possible to choose one a trifle higher or lower, but this one I consider the most accurate.

Now, to this declared fact that there are no more than thirty-six dramatic* situations, is attached a singular corollary, the discovery that there are in life but thirty-six emotions. A maximum of thirty-six emotions, —and therein we have all the savor of existence; there we have the unceasing ebb and flow which fills human history like tides of the sea; which is, indeed, the very substance of history, since it is the substance of humanity itself, in the shades of African forests as Unter den Linden or beneath the electric lights of the Boulevards; as it was in the ages of man's hand-to-hand struggle with the wild beasts of wood and mountain, and as it will be, indubitably, in the most infinitely distant future, since it is with these thirty-six emotions—no more— that we color, nay, we comprehend, cosmic mechanism, and since it is from them that our theogonies and our metaphysics are, and ever will be, constructed; all our dear and fanciful "beyonds;"—thirty-six situations, thirty-six emotions, and no more.

It is then, comprehensible that in viewing upon the stage the ceaseless mingling of these thirty-six emotions, a race or nation arrives at the beginning of its definite self-consciousness; the Greeks, indeed, began their towns by laying the foundations of a theater. It is equally nat-

---

* I have replaced the word "tragic," used in the quotation, with "dramatic." Those familiar with Goethe know that for him — one of the "classic" Germans — the two terms were synonymous in this passage.

ural that only the greatest and most complete civilizations should have evolved their own particular conception of the drama, and that one of these new conceptions should be revealed by each new evolution of society, whence arises the dim but faithful expectation of our own age, waiting for the manifestation of its own dramatic ideals, before the cenotaphs of an art which has long been, apparently for commercial reasons, almost non-existent.

In fine, after having brought together all these dramatic "points of view," we shall see, as in a panorama, the great procession of our race, in characteristic motley costumes: — Hindu kings in their chariots, Chinese gallants playing their mandores, nude heroes of Hellas, legendary knights, adventurers of sword and cape, golden-tressed princesses, nymphs sparkling with gems, shy maids with drooping eyelashes, famed courtesans, chaste Athenian virgins, priestly confessors, chattering gossips, gurus expounding religious ideas, satyrs leaping upon goats' feet, ugly slaves, peris, horned devils in disguise, lisping Tartaglias, garrulous Graciosos, Shakespearean clowns, Hugoesque buffoons, magistrates, immobile Buddhist ascetics, white-robed sacrificers, martyrs with shining aureoles, too-crafty Ulysses, frightful Rakchasas, messengers dispersing calamitous tidings to the winds of heaven, pure-hearted youths, blood-stained madmen, — yes, here it assembles, our humanity, here it moves through its periods of greatest intensity — but presenting always one of the facets of the prism possessed by Gozzi.

These thirty-six facets, which I have undertaken to recover, should obviously be simple and clean, and of no far-fetched character; of this we shall be convinced after seeing them repeated, with unfailing distinctness, in all epochs and in all genres. The reader will find, in my brief exposition, but twelve hundred examples cited, of which about a thousand are taken from the stage; but in this number I have included works the most dissimilar and the most celebrated, nearly all others being but mosaics of these. There will here be found the principal dramas of China, of India, of Judea, and, needless to say, of the Greek theater. However, instead of confining ourselves to the thirty-two classic tragedies we shall make use of those works of Hellenism which, unfortunately for the indolent public of today, still lie buried in Latin; works from whose great lines might be reconstructed hundreds of masterpieces, and all offering us, from the shades to which we have relegated them, the freshness of unfamiliar beauty. Leaving aside, for the present, any detailed consideration of the Persian and mediæval Mysteries, which depend almost without exception upon two or three situations, and which await a special study, we shall glance over, — after the Jeux and Miracles of the thirteenth and fourteenth centuries, — the Spanish authors, the French classics, the Italians, the Germans of the Romantic revival, and our modern dramatic literature. And it seems to me we shall have finally proved this theory of the Thirty-six Situations, when we shall thus have brought it into contact with the dramatic production of the last thirty years.

Two hundred of the examples cited have been taken from other literary genres akin to the dramatic: romance, epic, history, — and from reality. For this investigation can and should be pursued in human nature, by which I mean in politics, in courts of justice, in daily life. Amid these explorations the present study will soon seem but an introduction to a marvelous, an inexhaustible stream, — the Stream of Existence, where meet momentarily, in their primordial unity, history, mystic poetry, moralist (and amoralist) writings, humor, psychology, law, epic, romance, fable, myth, proverb and prophecy.

It may here be allowable to ask, with our theory in mind, a number of questions which to us are of primary importance.

Which are the dramatic situations neglected by our own epoch, so faithful in repeating the few most familiar? Which, on the other hand, are most in use today? Which are the most neglected, and which the most used, in each epoch, genre, school, author? What are the reasons for these preferences? The same questions may be asked before the classes and sub-classes of the situations.

Such an examination, which requires only patience,

will show first the list of combinations (situations and their classes and sub-classes) at present ignored, and which remain to be exploited in contemporaneous art, second, how these may be adapted. On the way it may chance that we shall discern, hidden within this or that one of our thirty-six categories, a unique case, — one without analogue among the other thirty-five, with no immediate relationship to any other, the product of a vigorous inspiration. But, in carefully determining the exact position of this case among the sub-classes of the situation to which it belongs, we shall be able to form, in each of the thirty-five others, a sub-class corresponding to it; thus will be created thirty-five absolutely new plots. These will give, when developed according to the taste of this or that school or period, a series of thirty-five "original imitations," thirty-five new scenarios, of a more unforeseen character, certainly, than the majority of our dramas, which, whether inspired by books or realities, when viewed in the clear light of the ancient writings revealed to us only their reflections, so long as we had not, for our guidance, the precious thread which vanished with Gozzi.

Since we now hold this thread, let us unwind it.

FIRST SITUATION

SUPPLICATION

(The dynamic elements technically necessary are: — a Persecutor, a Suppliant and a Power in authority, whose decision is doubtful.)

Among the examples here offered will be found those of three slightly differing classes. In the first, the power whose decision is awaited is a distinct personage, who is deliberating; shall he yield, from motives of prudence or from apprehension for those he loves, to the menaces of the persecutor, or rather, from generosity, to the appeal of the persecuted? In the second, by means of a contraction analogous to that which abbreviates a syllogism to an enthymeme, this undecided power is but an attribute of the persecutor himself, — a weapon suspended in his hand; shall anger or pity determine his course? In the third group, on the contrary, the suppliant element is divided between two persons, the Persecuted and the Intercessor, thus increasing the number of principal characters to four.

These three groups (A, B, C) may be subdivided as follows:

A (1) — **Fugitives Imploring the Powerful for Help Against Their Enemies.** — Complete examples: "The Suppliants" and "The Heraclidæ" of Aeschylus; "The Heraclidæ" of Euripides; the "Minos" of Sophocles. Cases in which the fugitives are guilty: the "Oïcles" and "Chryses" of Sophocles; "The Eumenides" of Aeschylus. A partial example: Act II of Shakespeare's "King John." Familiar instances: scenes from colonial protectorates.

13

(2) — **Assistance Implored for the Performance of a Pious Duty Which Has Been Forbidden.** — Complete examples: "The Eleusinians" of Aeschylus and "The Suppliants" of Euripides. A historical example: the burial of Molière. A familiar instance: a family divided in its religious belief, wherein a child, in order to worship according to his conscience, appeals to the parent who is his co-religionist.

(3) — **Appeals for a Refuge in Which to Die.** —Complete example: "Œdipus at Colonus." Partial example: the death of Zineb, in Hugo's "Mangeront-ils?"

B (1) — **Hospitality Besought by the Shipwrecked.** — Complete example: "Nausicaa" and "The Pheacians" of Sophocles. Partial example: Act I of Berlioz' "Trojans."

(2) — **Charity Entreated by Those Cast Off by Their Own People, Whom They Have Disgraced.** — Examples: the "Danae" of Aeschylus and the "Danae" of Euripides; the "Alope," "Auge" and "The Cretans" of Euripides. Familiar instances: a large part of the fifteen or twenty thousand adventures which, each year, come to an end in the Bureau des Enfants-Assistés. Special instance of a child received into a home: the beginning of "Le Rêve," by Zola.

(3) — **Expiation: The Seeking of Pardon, Healing or Deliverance.** — Examples: Sophocles' "Philoctetes;" Aeschylus' "Mysians;" Euripides' "Telephus;" "Les Champairol" (Rraisse, 1884). Historical example: the penitence of Barbarossa. Familiar instances: petitions for pardon, confession of Catholics, etc.

(4) — **The Surrender of a Corpse, or of a Relic, Solicited:** — "The Phrygians" of Aeschylus. Historical examples: the Crusaders' embassies to the Moslems. Familiar instances: the reclaiming of the remains of a great man buried in a foreign land; of the body of an executed person, or of a relative dead in a hospital. It should be noted that the "Phrygians," and the Twenty-fourth Book of the Iliad, which inspired the play, form a transition toward the Twelfth Situation (A Refusal Overcome).

C (1) — **Supplication of the Powerful for Those Dear**

to the Suppliant. — Complete example: Esther. Partial example: Margaret in the dénouement of "Faust." Historical example: Franklin at the court of Louis XVI. Example corresponding also to A (3): the "Propompes" of Aeschylus.

(2) — **Supplication to a Relative in Behalf of Another Relative.** — Example: the "Eurysaces" of Sophocles.

(3) — **Supplication to a Mother's Lover, in Her Behalf.** — Example: "L'Enfant de l'Amour" (Bataille, 1911).

It is apparent that, in the modern theater, very little use has been made of this First Situation. If we except subdivisions C (1), which is akin to the poetic cult of the Virgin and the Saints, and C (3), there is not a single pure example, doubtless for the reason that the antique models have disappeared or have become unfamiliar, and more particularly because, Shakespeare, Lope and Corneille not having transformed this theme or elaborated it with those external complexities demanded by our modern taste, their successors have found the First Situation too bare and simple a subject for this epoch. As if one idea were necessarily more simple than another! — as if all those which have since launched upon our stage their countless ramifications had not in the beginning shown the same vigorous simplicity!

It is, however, our modern predilection for the complex which, to my mind, explains the favor now accorded to group C alone, wherein by easy means a fourth figure (in essence, unfortunately, a somewhat parasitic and monotonous one), the Intercessor, is added to the trinity of Persecutor, Suppliant and Power.

Of what variety, nevertheless, is this trinity capable! The Persecutor, — one or many, voluntary or unconscious, greedy or revengeful, spreading the subtle network of diplomacy, or revealing himself beneath the formidable pomp of the greatest contemporary powers; the Suppliant, artless or eloquent, virtuous or guilty, humble or great; and the Power, neutral or partial to one side or the other, perhaps inferior in strength to the Persecutor and surrounded by his own kindred who fear danger, perhaps deceived by a semblance of right and justice, perhaps obliged to sacrifice a high ideal; sometimes severely logical, sometimes emotionally susceptible, or even overcome by a conversion a la Dostoievsky, and, as a final thunderbolt, abandoning the errors which he believed to be truth, if not indeed the truth which he believed to be error!

Nowhere, certainly, can the vicissitudes of power, be it arbitral, tyrannical, or overthrown, — the superstitions which may accompany doubt and indecision, — on the one side the sudden turns of popular opinion, on the other the anxiety with which they are awaited, — despairs and their resulting blasphemies, — hope surviving to the last breath, — the blind brutality of fate, — nowhere can they become so condensed and burst forth with such power as in this First Situation, in our day ignored.

France's enthusiastic sympathy for Poland, revived during the last half-century; the same sympathy which on so many historic occasions she has manifested for Scotland and for Ireland, might here find tragic expression; that cry of humanity with which a single priest, at the massacre of Fourmies, rallied to the Church a fraction of revolutionary France; the worship of the dead, that first, last, most primitive and most indestructible form of religious sentiment; the agony which awaits us all, agony dragging itself toward the darkness like a spent beast; the profoundly humble longing of one whom a murder has deprived of all that was dearest to him, that pitiable entreaty, on bended knees, which melted into tears the savage rancor of Achilles and caused him to forget his vow; — all are here in this First Situation, all these strong emotions, and yet others; nowhere else, indeed, can they be found in such completeness, — and our modern world of art has forgotten this situation!

SECOND SITUATION

DELIVERANCE

(Elements: an Unfortunate, a Threatener, a Rescuer)

This is, in a way, the converse of the First Situation, in which the unfortunate appeals to an undecided power, whereas here an unexpected protector, of his own accord, comes suddenly to the rescue of the distressed and despairing.

A — **Appearance of a Rescuer to the Condemned:** — The "Andromedas" of Sophocles, of Euripides and of Corneille; "Le Jeu de Saint Nicolas" (Jean Bodel). Partial examples: the first act of "Lohengrin;" the third act of Voltaire's "Tancred;" the role of the generous patron in "Boislaurier" (Richard, 1884). The last example and the following show particularly the honor of the unfortunate at stake: Daniel and Susanna, and various exploits of chivalry. A parody: "Don Quixote." A familiar instance: judicial assistance. The dénouement of "Bluebeard" (here the element of kinship enters, in the defense by brothers of their sister, and increases the pathos by the most simple of means, forgotten, however, by our playwrights).

B (1) — **A Parent Replaced Upon a Throne by His Children:** — "Aegeus" and "Peleus," by Sophocles; Euripides' "Antiope." Cases in which the children have previously been abandoned are "Athamas I" and also the "Tyro" of Sophocles. (The taste of the future author of "Œdipus at Colonus" for stories in which the Child plays the role of deliverer and dispenser of justice, forms

17

a bitter enough contrast to the fate which awaited the poet himself in his old age.)

(2) — Rescue by Friends, or by Strangers Grateful for Benefits or Hospitality: — Sophocles' "Œneus," "Iolas" and "Phineus." A partial example: the second part of Euripides' "Alceste." Example in comedy: Musset's "Fantasio." Example in which protection is accorded by the host who has granted asylum: Euripides' "Dictys."

We see, by a glance over these subdivisions, what our writers might have drawn from the second of the Situations. For us, indeed, it should possess some little attraction, if only for the reason that two thousand years ago humanity once more listened to this story of the Deliverer, and since then has so suffered, loved and wept for the sake of it. This situation is also the basis of Chivalry, that original and individual heroism of the Middle Ages; and, in a national sense, of the French Revolution. Despite all this, in art, — if we except the burlesque of Cervantes, and the transplendent light flashing from the silver armor of Lohengrin, — in art, as yet, it is hardly dreamed of.

THIRD SITUATION

CRIME PURSUED BY VENGEANCE

(Elements: an Avenger and a Criminal)

Vengeance is a joy divine, says the Arab; and such indeed it seems to have frequently been, to the God of Israel. The two Homeric poems both end with an intoxicating vengeance, as does the characteristic Oriental legend of the Pandavas; while to the Latin and Spanish races the most satisfying of spectacles is still that of an individual capable of executing a legitimate, although illegal, justice. So much goes to prove that even twenty centuries of Christianity, following five centuries of Socratic philosophy, have not sufficed to remove Vengeance from its pedestal of honor, and to substitute thereon Pardon. And Pardon itself, even though sincere, — what is it but the subtle quintessence of vengeance upon earth, and at the same time the claiming of a sort of wergild from Heaven?

A (1) — **The Avenging of a Slain Parent or Ancestor:** — "The Singer," an anonymous Chinese drama; "The Tunic Confronted" (of the courtesan Tchangkouepin); "The Argives" and "The Epigones" of Aeschylus; Sophocles' "Aletes and Erigone;" "The Two Foscari," by Byron; Werner's "Attila;" "Le Crime de Maison-Alfort" (Coedes, 1881); "Le Maquignon" (Josz and Dumur, 1903). In the last three cases, as well as in the following one, the vengeance is accomplished not by a son, but by a daughter. Example from fiction: Mérimée's "Colomba." Familiar instances: the majority of vendettas. "Le Prêtre" (Buet, 1881) presents especially the psychologic struggle between pardon and vengeance. Example of the avenging of a father driven to suicide: "L'Or" (Peter and Danceny, 1908).

(2) — **The Avenging of a Slain Child or Descendant:** — Sophocles' "Nauplius;" a part of "Sainte-Helene" (Mme. Séverine, 1902); the end of Euripides' "Hecuba." Epic example: Neptune's pursuit of Ulysses because of the blinding of Polyphemus.

(3) — **Vengeance for a Child Dishonored:** — "El Mejor Alcalde el Rey," by Lope de Vega; "The Alcalde of Zalamea," by Calderon. Historic example: the death of Lucrece.

(4) — **The Avenging of a Slain Wife or Husband:** — Carneille's "Pompée;" "L'Idiot" (de Lorde, 1903). Contemporary instance: the trials of Mme. Veuve Barrême.

(5) — **Vengeance for the Dishonor, or Attempted Dishonoring, of a Wife:** — The "Ixion" of Aeschylus, of Sophocles and of Euripides; "The Perrhoebides" of Aeschylus; "Les Révoltés" (Cain and Adenis, 1908). Historic example: the priest of Ephraim. Similar cases, in which the wife has only been insulted: "Venisamhâra," by Bhatta Narayana; "The Sons of Pandou," by Rajasekhara. Familiar instances: a large number of duels.

(6) — **Vengeance for a Mistress Slain:** — "Love after Death," by Caleron; "Amhra" (Grangeneuve, 1882); "Simon the Foundling" (Jonathan, 1882).

(7) — **Vengeance for a Slain or Injured Friend:** — "The Nereids" of Aeschylus. A contemporary instance: Ravachol. Case in which the vengeance is perpetrated upon the mistress of the avenger: "La Casserole" (Méténier, 1889).

(8) — **Vengeance for a Sister Seduced:** — Goethe's "Clavijo;" "Les Bouchers" (Icres, 1888); "La Casquette au Pere Bugeaud" (Marot, 1886). Examples from fiction: "La Kermesse Rouge," in Eekhoud's collection, and the end of Bourget's "Disciple."

B (1) — **Vengeance for Intentional Injury or Spolia-**

tion: — Shakespeare's "Tempest." Contemporary instance: Bismarck in his retirement at Varzin.

(2) — **Vengeance for Having Been Despoiled During Absence:** — "Les Joueurs d'Osselets" and "Penelope," by Aeschylus; "The Feast of the Achaeans," by Sophocles.

(3) — **Revenge for an Attempted Slaying:** — "The Anger of Te-oun-go," by Kouan-han-king. A similar case involving at the same time the saving of a loved one by a judicial error: "La Cellule No. 7" (Zaccone, 1881).

(4) — **Revenge for a False Accusation:** — T h e "Phrixus" of Sophocles and of Euripides; Dumas' "Monte-Cristo;" "La Declassee" (Delahaye, 1883); "Roger-la-Honte" (Mary, 1881).

(5) — **V e n g e a n c e f o r Violation:** — Sophocles' "Tereus;" "The Courtesan of Corinth" (Carré and Bilhaud, 1908); "The Cenci," by Shelley (parricide as the punishment of incest).

(6) — **Vengeance for Having Been Robbed of One's Own:** — "The Merchant of Venice," and partly "William Tell."

(7) — **Revenge Upon a Whole Sex for a Deception by One:** — "Jack the Ripper" (Bertrand and Clairian, 1889); the fatal heroines of the typical plays of the Second Empire, "L'Etrangère," etc. A case appertaining also to Class A: the motive (an improbable one) of the corruptress in "Possédé," by Lemonnier.

We here encounter for the first time that grimacing personage who forms the keystone of all drama dark and mysterious, — the "villain." About the beginning of our Third Situation we might evoke him at every step, this villain and his profound schemes which not infrequently make us smile. Don Salluste in "Ruy-Blas," Iago in "Othello," Guanhumara in "Burgraves," Homodei in "Angelo," Mahomet in the tragedy of that name, Leontine in "Heraclius," Maxime in "La Tragedie de Valentinien," Emire in "Siroès," Ulysses in "Palamedes."

C — **Professional Pursuit of Criminals** (the counterpart of which will be found in the Fifth Situation, Class A): — "Sherlock Holmes" (Conan Doyle); "Vidocq"

(Bergerat, 1910); "Nick Carter" (Busson and Livet, 1910).

Frequently used though this situation has been in our day, many an ancient case awaits its rejuvenescence, many a gap is yet to be filled. Indeed, among the bonds which may unite avenger and victim, more than one degree of relationship has been omitted, as well as the majority of social and business ties. The list of wrongs which might provoke reprisal is far from being exhausted, as we may assure ourselves by enumerating the kinds of offenses possible against persons or property, the varying shades of opinion of opposing parties, the different ways in which an insult may take effect, and how many and what sort of relationships may exist between Avenger and Criminal. And these questions concern merely the premises of the action.

To this we may add all the turns and bearings, slow or instantaneous, direct or tortuous, frantic or sure, which punishment can take, the thousand resources which it offers, the points at which it may aim in its deadly course, the obstacles which chance or the defendant may present. Next introduce various secondary figures, each pursuing his own aims, as in life, intercrossing each other and crossing the drama — and I have sufficient esteem for the reader's capabilities to develop the subject no further.

FOURTH SITUATION

VENGEANCE TAKEN FOR KINDRED UPON KINDRED

(Elements: Avenging Kinsman; Guilty Kinsman; Remembrance of the Victim, a Relative of Both.)

Augmenting the horror of Situation XXVII ("Discovery of the Dishonor of One's Kindred") by the rough vigor of Situation III, we create the present action, which confines itself to family life, making of it a worse hell than the dungeon of Poe's "Pit and the Pendulum." The horror of it is such that the terrified spectators dare not intervene; they seem to be witnessing at a distance some demoniac scene silhouetted in a flaming house.

Neither, it seems, do our dramatists dare intervene to modify the Greek tragedy, — such as it is after thirty appalling centuries.

For us it is easy to compute, from the height of our "platform" — to use Gozzi's word — the infinite variations possible to this theme, by multiplying the combinations which we have just found in the Third Situation, by those which the Twenty-seventh will give us.

Other germs of fertility will be found in turn in the circumstances which have determined the avenger's action. These may be a spontaneous desire on his own part (the simplest motive); the wish of the dying victim, or of the spirit of the dead mysteriously appearing to the living; an imprudent promise; a professional duty (as when the avenger is a magistrate, etc.); the necessity of saving other relatives or a beloved one (thus did Talien

avenge the Dantonists) or even fellow-citizens; ignorance of the kinship which exists between Avenger and
Criminal. There yet remains that case in which the
Avenger strikes without having recognized the Criminal
(in a dark room, I suppose); the case in which the act of
intended vengeance is but the result of an error, the sup-
posedly guilty kinsman being found innocent, and his
pseudo-executioner discovering that he has but made of
himself a detestable criminal.

A (1) — A Father's Death Avenged Upon a Mother:
—"The Choephores" of Aeschylus; the "Electras" of
Sophocles, Euripides, Attilius, Q. Cicero, Pradon, Longe-
pierre, Crébillon, Rochefort, Chénier, and of Guillard's
opera; the "Orestes" of Voltaire and of Alfieri; Sophocles' "Epigones;" the "Eriphyles" of Sophocles and of
Voltaire; and lastly "amlet," in which we recognize so
clearly the method by which the poet rejuvenates his
subjects, — by an almost antithetic change of characters
and of milieu.

(2) — A Mother Avenged Upon a Father: — "Zoe
Chien-Chien" (Matthey, 1881), in which the parricide is
counterbalanced by an incestuous passion, and is committed by the daughter, not by the son.

B — A Brother's Death Avenged Upon a Son (but
without premeditation, this accordingly falling almost
into the situation "Imprudence"): — Aeschylus' "Ata-
lanta" and Sophocles' "Meleager."

C — A Father's Death Avenged Upon a Husband: —
"Rosmunde" (Rucellai).

D — A Husband's Death Avenged Upon a Father: —
"Orbecche" by Giraldi.

Thus, of twenty-two works, eighteen are in the same
class, seventeen in the same sub-class, thirteen upon the
same subject; — four classes and one sub-class altogether. Let us, for the moment, amuse ourselves by
counting some of those which have been forgotten.

A father's death avenged upon the brother of the
avenger. Upon his sister. Upon his mistress (or, in the
case of a feminine avenger, upon her lover, for each of
the cases enumerated has its double, according to the

sex of the avenger). Upon his wife. Upon his son. Upon his daughter. Upon his paternal uncle. Upon his maternal uncle. Upon his paternal or maternal grandfather; his paternal or maternal grandmother. Upon half-brother or half-sister. Upon a person allied by marriage (brother-in-law, sister-in-law, etc.) or a cousin. These numerous variations may of course be successively repeated for each case: — the avenging of a brother, a sister, a husband, a son, a grandfather, and so on.

By way of variety, the vengeance may be carried out, not upon the person of the criminal himself, but upon some one dear to him (thus Medea and Atreus struck Jason and Thyestes through their children), and even inanimate objects may take the place of victims.

FIFTH SITUATION

PURSUIT

(Elements: Punishment and Fugitive)

As the Second Situation was the converse of the First, so this situation of Pursuit represents a transition into the passive of the Third and Fourth, and, in fact, of all those in which danger pursues a character. There remains, however, a distinction; in Pursuit the avenging elements hold second place, or perhaps not even that; it may be, indeed, quite invisible and abstract. Our interest is held by the fugitive alone; sometimes innocent, always excusable, for the fault — if there was one — appears to have been inevitable, ordained; we do not inquire into it or blame it, which would be idle, but sympathetically suffer the consequences with our hero, who, whatever he may once have been, is now but a fellow-man in danger. We recall that truth which Goethe once flung in the face of hypocrisy; that, each one of us having within him the potentiality for all the crimes, there is not one which it is impossible to imagine ourselves committing, under certain circumstances. In this Situation we feel ourselves, so to speak, accomplices in even the worst of slayings. Which may be explained by the reflection that along our various lines of heredity many such crimes might be found, and our present virtuousness may mean simply an immunity from criminal tendencies which we have gained by the experience of our ancestors. If this be the case, heredity and environment, far from being oppressive fatalities, become the germs of wisdom, which,

satiety being reached, will triumph. This is why genius
(not that of neurosis, but of the more uncommon mas-
tery of neurosis) appears especially in families which
have transmitted to it a wide experience of folly.

Through drama, then, we are enabled to gain our experience of error and catastrophe in a less costly way;
by means of it we evoke vividly the innumerable memories which are sleeping in our blood, that we may purify
ourselves of them by force of repetition, and accustom
our dark souls to their own reflections. Like music, it
will in the end "refine our manners" and dower us with
the power of self-control, basis of all virtue. Nothing
is more moral in effect than immorality in literature.

The sense of isolation which characterizes Situation
V gives a singular unity to the action, and a clear field
for psychologic observation, which need not be lessened
by diversity of scenes and events.

A — Fugitives from Justice Pursued for Brigandage,
Political Offenses, Etc.: — "Louis Perez of Galicia" and
"Devotion to the Cross," both by Calderon; the beginning of the mediæval Miracle "Robert-le-Diable;" "The
Brigands" by Schiller; "Raffles" (Hornung, 1907). Historical examples: the proscription of the Conventionnels;
the Duchesse de Berry. Examples from fiction: "Rocam-
bole" by Gaboriau; "Arsène Lupin" (Leblanc). Familiar
instances: police news. Example in comedy: "Compère
le Renard" (Polti, 1905).

B — Pursued for a Fault of Love: — Unjustly, "In-
digne!" (Barbier, 1884); more justly, Molière's "Don
Juan" and Corneille's "Festin de Pierre," (not to speak
of various works of Tirso de Molina, Tellez, Villiers,
Sadwell, Zamora, Goldoni, Grabbe, Zorilla, Dumas père);
very justly, "Ajax of Locris," by Sophocles. Familiar
instances run all the way from the forced marriage of
seducers to arrests for sidewalk flirtations.

C — A Hero Struggling Against a Power: — Aeschylus' "Prometheus Bound;" Sophocles' "Laocoon;" the
role of Porus in Racine's and also in Metastasio's "Alex-
andre;" Corneille's "Nicomede;" Goethe's "Goetz von
Berlichingen" and a part of "Egmont;" Metastasio's

"Cato;" Manzoni's "Adelghis" and a part of his "Count of Carmagnola;" the death of Hector in Shakespeare's "Troilus and Cressida;" "Nana-Sahib" (Richepin, 1883); "Edith" (Bois, 1885); the tetralogy of the "Nibelungen;" "An Enemy of the People" (Ibsen); "Le Roi sans Couronne" (de Bouhélier, 1909).

D — A Pseudo-Madman Struggling Against an Iago-Like Alienist: — "La Vicomtesse Alice" (Second 1882).

SIXTH SITUATION

DISASTER

(Elements: a Vanquished Power; a Victorious Enemy
or a Messenger)

Fear, catastrophe, the unforeseen; a great reversal of
rôles; the powerful are overthrown, the weak exalted.
Here is the oft-recurring refrain of the Biblical books,
here the immortal echoes of the fall of Troy, at which
we still pale as though with a presentiment.

A (1) — **Defeat Suffered:** — "The Myrmidons" and
"The Persians" of Aeschylus; "The Shepherds" of Soph-
ocles. Example from fiction: "La Debâcle," by Zola.
History is made up of repetitions of this story.

(2) — **A Fatherland Destroyed:** — T h e "X o a n e-
phores" of Sophocles; Byron's "Sardanapalus" (this
corresponds also to Class B, and toward the dénouement
recalls the Fifth Situation). Examples from history:
Poland; the great Invasions. From romance: "The War
of the Worlds" (Wells).

(3) — **The Fall of Humanity:** — The Mystery of
"Adam" (twelfth century).

(4) — **A Natural Catastrophe:** — "T e r r e d'Epou-
vante" (de Lorde and Morel, 1907).

B — **A Monarch Overthrown** (the converse of the
Eighth) : — Shakespeare's "Henry VI" and "Richard
II." Historic instances: Charles I, Louis XVI, Napo-
leon, etc.; and, substituting other authorities than kings,
Colomb, de Lesseps. and all disgraced ministers. Ex-

amples from fiction: the end of "Tartarin," "L'Argent," "Cesar Birotteau."

C (1) — **Ingratitude Suffered** (of all the blows of misfortune, this is perhaps the most poignant): — Euripides' "Archelaus" (excepting the dénouement, in which the action is reversed); Shakespeare's "Timon of Athens" and "King Lear," and the beginning of his "Coriolanus;" Byron's "Marino Faliero;" a part of "The Count of Carmagnola," by Manzoni. Bismarck's dismissal by the young Emperor William. The martyrs, the many instances of devotion and sacrifice unappreciated by those who have benefited by it, the most glorious of deaths shine against this dark background; Socrates and the Passion are but the most celebrated examples. "Le Reformateur" (Rod, 1906).

(2) — **The Suffering of Unjust Punishment or Enmity** (this corresponds in some degree to the "Judicial Errors"): — Sophocles' "Teucer;" Aeschylus' Salaminiae."

(3) — **An Outrage Suffered:** — the first act of "The Cid;" the first act of "Lucrece Borgia." The "point of honor" offers better material than these simple episodes. We may imagine some more sensitive Voltaire, reduced by his persecutions to helplessness and to the point of dying in despair.

D (1) — **Abandonment by a Lover or a Husband:** — "Faust;" Corneille's "Ariane;" the beginning of the "Medeas;" "Maternite" (Brieux, 1903).

(2) — **Children Lost by Their Parents:** — "Le Petit Poucet."

If Classes B, C and D, which are concerned with the fate of individuals, have been so much less developed than they might easily have been, what shall be said of the case of social disasters, such as Class A? Shakespeare did not tread far enough upon that majestic way. Only among the Greeks has a work of this kind presented at one stroke that conception of human events, sublime, fatalistic and poetic, of which Herodotus was one day to create history.

SEVENTH SITUATION

FALLING PREY TO CRUELTY OR MISFORTUNE

(Elements: an Unfortunate; a Master or a Misfortune)

To infinite sorrow there is no limit. Beneath that which seems the final depth of misfortune, there may open another yet more frightful. A ferocious and deliberate dissection of the heart it seems, this Seventh Situation, — that of pessimism par excellence.

A — **The Innocent Made the Victim of Ambitious Intrigue:** — "The Princess Maleine" (Maeterlinck); "The Natural Daughter," by Goethe; "Les Deux Jumeaux," by Hugo.

B — **The Innocent Despoiled by Those Who Should Protect:** — "The Guests" and the beginning of the "Joueurs d'Osselets," by Aeschylus (at the first vibration of the great bow in the hands of the unknown Beggar, what a breath of hope we draw!); "Les Corbeaux," by Becque; "Le Roi de Rome" (Pouvillon); "L'Aiglon" (Rostand); "La Croisade des Enfantelets Francs" (Ernault).

C (1) — **The Powerful Dispossessed and Wretched:** — The beginning of Sophocles' and of Euripides' "Peleus;" of "Prometheus Bound;" of "Job." Laertes in his garden. Example from comedy: "Le Jeu de la Feuillée" (Adam de la Halle).

(2) — **A Favorite or an Intimate Finds Himself Forgotten:** — "En Détresse" (Fevre, 1890).

D — **The Unfortunate Robbed of Their Only Hope:** — "The Blind," by Maeterlinck; "Beethoven" (Fauchois, 1909) ; "Rembrandt" (Dumur and Josz).

And how many cases yet remain! The Jews in captivity, slavery in America, the Horrors of the Hundred Years' War, invaded ghettos, scenes such as draw the crowd to any reproduction of prison life or of Inquisition, the attraction of Dante's Inferno, of Pellico's "Prisons," the transporting bitterness of Gautama, of Ecclesiastes, of Schopenhauer!

EIGHTH SITUATION

REVOLT

(Elements: Tyrant and Conspirator)

As already observed, this situation is, in a measure, the converse of Class B of Situation VI.

Intrigue, so dear to the public of the past three centuries, is obviously supplied by the very nature of the subject we are now to consider. But, by some strange chance, it has, on the contrary, always been treated with the most open candor and simplicity. One or two vicissitudes, a few surprises all too easily foreseen and extending uniformly to all the personages of the play, and there we have the conditions which have almost invariably been attached to this action, so propitious, nevertheless, to doubts, to equivocation, to a twilight whose vague incertitude prepares the dawn of revolt and of liberty.

A (1) — **A Conspiracy Chiefly of One Individual:** — "The Conspiracy of Fiesco," by Schiller; Corneille's "Cinna;" to some extent the "Catilina" of Voltaire (this tragedy belongs rather to the Thirtieth Situation, "Ambition"); "Thermidor;" "The Conspiracy of General Malet" (Augé de Lassus, 1889); "Le Grand Soir" (Kampf); "Le Roi sans Royaume" (Decourcelle, 1909): "Lorenzaccio" (Musset).

(2) — **A Conspiracy of Several:** — "The Conspiracy of the Pazzi" by Alfieri;" Le Roman d'une Conspiration" (by Fournier and Carré, after the story of Ranc); "Madame Margot" (Moreau and Clairville, 1909); and,

in comedy, "Chantecler" (Rostand, 1910) with its parody
"Rosse, tant et plus" (Mustière, 1910).

B (1) — **Revolt of One Individual, Who Influences
and Involves Others:** — Goethe's "Egmont;" "Jacques
Bonhomme" (Maujan, 1886); "La Mission de Jeanne
d'Arc" (Dallierè, 1888). Example from fiction: "Salammbô." From history: Solon feigning madness.

(2) — **A Revolt of Many:** — "Fontovejune," by Lope
de Vega; Schiller's "William Tell;" Zola's "Germinal;"
"The Weavers of Silesia," by Hauptmann (forbidden in
1893 with the approval of a Parliament soon afterward
dissolved); "L'Automne," by Paul Adam and Gabriel
Mourey (forbidden in 1893 with the approval of another
Parliament shortly before its dissolution); "L'Armée
dans la Ville" (Jules Romain, 1911): "The Fourteenth
of July" (Roland, 1902). From fiction: a part of the
"Fortunes des Rougon" by Zola. From history: the
taking of the Bastile, and numerous disturbances of the
same period.

This species of action, particularly in modern scenes,
has given fine virile dramas to England, Spain, Italy and
Germany; of a forceful and authoritative character in the
two first countries, of a youthful enthusiastic type in the
two last. France, most certainly, would seem of all
countries the most likely to understand and express such
emotions.

But . . . "Thermidor" was prohibited "for fear"
it might offend the friends (centenarians apparently) of
Maximilian; "Le Pater" "for fear" it might be displeas-
ing to Communists; Zola's "Germinal" and "L'Automne"
by Adam and Mourey (two works painted in widely
different colors, as the titles sufficiently indicate) were
stopped "for fear" of the objections of a few conserva-
tives; "Other People's Money" by Hennique, "for fear"
of shocking certain financiers who have since been put
behind bars; "Lohengrin" (although the subject is
Celtic) was long forbidden "for fear" of irritating a half-
dozen illiterate French chauvinists; an infinite number
of other plays "for fear" of annoying Germany (or our

parlor diplomats who talk of it). . . . Yet others "for fear" of vexing the Grand Turk!

Is it possible, notwithstanding all this, to find a single instance in which a dramatic production has brought about a national calamity such as our censors fear? The pretext is no more sincere than are those urged for excluding from the theater any frank and truthful representations of love. A rule against admitting children should be sufficient to satisfy modesty on this point; even that is little needed, since children unaccompanied by their elders rarely apply for admission.

Our sentimental bourgeoisie apparently holds to the eighteenth-century opinion that it is more dangerous to listen to these things in public than to read of them in private. For our dramatic art — which, be it noted, has remained, despite its decline, the one great unrivalled means of propagating French thought t h r o u g h o u t Europe — has been forbidden, little by little, to touch directly upon theology, politics, sociology, upon criminals or crimes, excepting (and pray why this exception?) adultery, upon which subject our theater, to its great misfortune, now lives, at least two days out of three.

The ancients had a saying that a man enslaved loses half his soul. A dramatist is a man.

NINTH SITUATION

DARING ENTERPRISE

(A Bold Leader; an Object; an Adversary)

The Conflict, which forms the framework of all dramatic situations, is, in the Ninth, clearly drawn, undisguised. A clever plan, a bold attempt, sangfroid, — and victory!

A — **Preparations For War:** — (In this class, as anciently treated, the action stops before the dénouement, which it leaves to be imagined, in the perspective of enthusiastic p r e d i c t i o n). Examples: — Aeschylus' "Nemea;" "The Council of the Argives" by Sophocles. Historic examples: the call to the Crusades; the Volunteers of '92.

B (1) — **War:** — Shakespeare's "Henry V."

(2) — **A Combat:** — "Glaucus Pontius," "Memnon," "Phineus" and "The Phorcides" of Aeschylus.

C (1) — **Carrying Off a Desired Person or Object:** — the "Prometheus" of Aeschylus; the "Laconian Women," by Sophocles. From fiction: the taking of the Zaimph in "Salammbô." Epic example: the second Homeric hymn (to Hermes).

(2) — **Recapture of a Desired Object:** — "The Victory of Arjuna," by Cantchana Atcharya; Wagner's "Parsifal;" the retaking of the Zaimph.

D (1) — **Adventurous Expeditions:** — Lope's "Discovery of the New World;" Aeschylus' "Prometheus Unbound;" Euripides' "Theseus;" Sophocles' "Sinon;"

the "Rhesus" attributed to Euripides. Examples from romance: the usual exploits of the heroes of fairy tales; the Labors of Hercules; the majority of Jules Verne's stories.

(2) — **Adventure Undertaken for the Purpose of Obtaining a Beloved Woman:** — Sophocles' and Euripides' "Œnomaüs." From fiction: "Toilers of the Sea." For the purpose of saving the honor of a lover: "La Petite Caporale" (Darlay and de Gorsse, 1909).

The Ninth Situation thus summarizes the poetry of war, of robbery, of surprise, of desperate chance, — the poetry of the clear-eyed adventurer, of man beyond the restraints of artificial civilizations, of Man in the original acceptation of the term. We find, nevertheless, hardly a single French work in this class!

Lest the reader be wearied, I refrain from enumerating, under these classes so lightly touched upon, many of the plots and complications which might be evolved from them. Methods of tracking the human game — bandit or hero, — the forces conspiring for his disaster, the conditions which make him the victim of his masters, the ways in which revolt may arise, the alternatives of the struggle in a "daring enterprise," certainly would appear to be more complex today than in earlier ages; moreover, upon these themes parts borrowed from other situations may be engrafted with remarkable ease. Even if we desire to preserve to the said themes their archaic severity, how much may yet be drawn from them! In how many ways, to cite but one example, might an Adventurous Expedition be changed by varying the motives or the object of the enterprise, the nature of the obstacles, the qualities of the hero, and the previous bearings of the three indispensable elements of the drama! "Adventurous Travels" have hardly been touched upon. And how many other classes are there which have not been!

TENTH SITUATION

ABDUCTION

(The Abductor; the Abducted; the Guardian)

Or, the Great Bourgeois Romance! Was it not thus that Molière used to put an end to his comedies, when he judged that the moment had arrived for sending his audience home satisfied? Sometimes he substituted a treasure-box for a girl, as in "Tartuffe," or arranged an exchange of the one for the other, as in "L'Avare."

We find in ABDUCTION one of the situations bearing upon Rivalry, and in which Jealousy appears, although not painted with so superb a coloring as in the Twenty-fourth.

In two of the following classes (B and C) we may remark the intrusion of the situations "Adultery" and "Recovery of a Lost Loved One." The same usage is quite possible in almost all the other situations. I would point out to those who may be interested in a more detailed analysis, that love is not necessarily the motive of Abduction (in Class D will be found friendship, faith, etc.) nor the reason of the obstacles raised by the guardian.

A — **Abduction of an Unwilling Woman:** — Aeschylus' and Sophocles' "Orithyies;" Aeschylus' "Europa" and "The Carians." "With Fire and Sword" (after Sienkiewicz, 1904). Comedy: "Le Jeu de Robin et de Marion" (Adam de la Halle). Historic and legendary: the Sabine women; Cassandra. There appears to me to be tragic material in cases of extreme eroticism, of premeditated violation preceded by a mania of passion and its resulting state of overexcitation, and followed by the murder of the outraged victim, by regrets before the beautiful corpse, by the repugnant work of dismemberment or concealment of the body; then by a disgust for life and by successive blunders which lead to the discovery of the criminal.

B — **Abduction of a Consenting Woman:** — "T h e Abduction of Helen" by Sophocles, and the comedy of the same name but not upon the same subject, by Lope. Numberless other comedies and romances.

C (1) — **Recapture of the Woman Without the Slaying of the Abductor:** — Euripides' "Helen;" "Malati and Madhava," by Bhavabhuti (the poet "of voice divine"). Rescue of a sister: "Iphigenia in Tauris."

(2) — **The Same Case, with the Slaying of the Ravisher:** — "Mahaviracharita," by Bhavabhuti; "Hanouman" (a collaborative work); "Anarghara-ghava" (anonymous); "The Message of Angada," by Soubhata; "Abhirama Mani," by Soundara Misra; "Hermione" by Sophocles.

D (1) — **Rescue of a Captive Friend:** — "Richard Coeur-de-Lion," by Sedaine and Gretry. A great number of escapes, historic and fictitious.

(2) — **Of a Child:** — "L'Homme de Proie" (Lefevre and Laporte, 1908).

(3) — **Of a Soul in Captivity to Error:** — "Barlaam and Josaphat," a fourteenth-century Miracle. The deeds of the Apostles, of missionaries, etc.

ELEVENTH SITUATION

THE ENIGMA

(Interrogator, Seeker and Problem)

This situation possesses theatrical interest par excellence, since the spectator, his curiosity aroused by the problem, easily becomes so absorbed as to fancy it is himself who is actually solving it. A combat of the intelligence with opposing wills, the Eleventh Situation may be fitly symbolized by an interrogation point.

A — **Search for a Person Who Must Be Found on Pain of Death:** — Sophocles' and Euripides' "Polyidus." Case without this danger, in which an object, not a person, is sought: Poe's "Purloined Letter."

B (1) — **A Riddle to Be Solved on Pain of Death:** — "The Sphinx" of Aeschylus. Example from fiction (without the danger): "The Gold Bug" by Poe.

(2) — **The Same Case, in Which the Riddle is Proposed by the Coveted Woman:** — Partial example: the beginning of Shakespeare's "Pericles." Example from fiction: "The Travelling Companion," by Andersen. Epic example (but without the danger): the Queen of Sheba and Solomon. Partial example: Portia's coffers, in "The Merchant of Venice."

The sort of contest, preliminary to the possession of a desired one, which is vaguely sketched in this episode, is singularly alluring in its suggestive analogues. But how many fibres, ready to thrill, will the perplexities of the love contest find in us, when they are raised to their third power by the introduction of the terrible, as in the one complete and pure example which we have, — the "Turandot" of the incomparable Gozzi; a work passionately admired, translated, produced and rendered famous in Germany by Schiller; a work which has for a century been regarded as a classic by all the world, although it remains little known in France.

The effect of B (2) is strengthened and augmented in cases in which the hero is subjected to the following:

C (1) — **Temptations Offered With the Object of Discovering His Name.**

(2) — **Temptations Offered With the Object of Ascertaining the Sex:** — "The Scyrian Women" of Sophocles and of Euripides.

(3) — **Tests for the Purpose of Ascertaining the Mental Condition:** — "Ulysses Furens" of Sophocles; "The Palamedes" of Aeschylus and of Euripides (according to the themes attributed to these lost works). Examinations of criminals by alienists.

TWELFTH SITUATION

OBTAINING

(A Solicitor and an Adversary Who is Refusing, or an Arbitrator and Opposing Parties)

Diplomacy and eloquence here come into play. An end is to be attained, an object to be gained. What interests may not be put at stake, what weighty arguments or influences removed, what intermediaries or disguises may be used to transform anger into benevolence, rancor into renouncement; to put the Despoiler in the place of the Despoiled? What mines may be sprung, what counter-mines discovered! — what unexpected revolts of submissive instruments! This dialectic contest which arises between reason and passion, sometimes subtile and persuasive, sometimes forceful and violent, provides a fine situation, as natural as it is original.

A — **Efforts to Obtain an Object by Ruse or Force:** — the "Philoctetes" of Aeschylus, of Sophocles and of Euripides; the reclamation of the Thebans in "Œdipus at Colonus;" "The Minister's Ring," by Vishakadatta.

B — **Endeavor by Means of Persuasive Eloquence Alone:** — "The Desert Isle," by Metastasio; the father's attitude in "Le Fils Naturel" (Dumas), to which Ruse is soon afterward added; Scene 2 of Act V of Shakespeare's "Coriolanus."

C — **Eloquence With an Arbitrator:** — "The Judgment of Arms," by Aeschylus; "Helen Reclaimed," by Sophocles.

One of the cases unused in the theater, notwithstanding its frequency, is Temptation, already introduced as a part of the preceding situation. The irritated adversary is here the Defiant; the solicitor, now the Tempter, has undertaken an unusual negotiation, one for the obtaining of an object which nothing can persuade the ower to part with; consequently the aim must be, gently, little by little, to bewilder, charm or stupefy him. Eternal rôle of woman toward man! — and of how many things toward the project of being a man! Does it not call to mind the hieratic attitude of the Christian toward Satan, as Flaubert has illuminated it, with a thousand sparkling lights, in his "Temptation of Saint Anthony?"

THIRTEENTH SITUATION

ENMITY OF KINSMEN

(Elements: a Malevolent Kinsman; a Hated or
Reciprocally Hating Kinsman)

Antithesis, which constituted for Hugo the gener-
ative principle of art, — dramatic art in particular, —
and which naturally results from the idea of Conflict
which is the basis of drama, offers one of the most symmetrical of schemes in these contrasting emotions.
"Hatred of one who should be loved," of which the
worthy pendant is the Twenty-Ninth, "Love of one who
should be hated." Such confluents necessarily give rise
to stormy action.

It is easy to foresee the following laws:

First: The more closely are drawn the bonds which
unite kinsmen at enmity, the more savage and dangerous their outbursts of hate are rendered.

Second: When the hatred is mutual, it will better
characterize our Situation than when it exists upon one
side only, in which case one of the relatives becomes
Tyrant and the other Victim, the ensemble resulting in
Situations V, VII, VIII, XXX, etc.

Third: The great difficulty will be to find and to
represent convincingly an element of discord powerful
enough to cause the breaking of the strongest human
ties.

A — **Hatred of Brothers: (1) — One Brother Hated
by Several** (the hatred not malignant): "The Heliades"

of Aeschylus (motive, envy) ; "The Labors of Jacob," by Lope de Vega (motive, filial jealousy). Hated by a single brother: The "Phoenissae" of Euripides and of Seneca; "Polynices" by Alfieri (motive, tyrannical avarice) ; Byron's "Cain" (motive, religious jealousy) ; "Une Famille au Temps de Luther" by Delavigne (motive, religious dissent) ; "Le Duel" (Lavedan, 1905).

(2) — Reciprocal Hatred: — The "Seven Against Thebes," by Aeschylus, and "Les Frères Ennemis" by Racine (motive, greed for power) ; an admirable supplementary character is added in this Theban legend, the Mother, torn between the sons; "Thyestes II" of Sophocles; "Thyestes" of Seneca; the "Pelopides" by Voltaire; "Atreus and Thyestes" by Crébillon (motive, greed for power, the important rôle being that of the perfidious instigator).

(3) — Hatred Between Relatives for Reasons of Self-Interest: — "La Maison d'Argile" (Fabre, 1907). Example from fiction: "Mon Frère" (Mercereau).

B — Hatred of Father and Son: — (1) — Of the Son for the Father: — "Three Punishments in One," by Calderon. Historic example: Louis XI and Charles VII. A part of "La Terre" by Zola and of "Le Maitre" by Jean Jullien.

(2) — Mutual Hatred: — "Life is a Dream," by Calderon. Historic instance: Jerome and Victor Bonaparte (a reduction of hatred to simple disagreement). This nuance appears to me to be one of the finest, although one of the least regarded by our writers.

(3) — Hatred of Daughter for Father: — "T h e Cenci," by Shelley (parricide as a means of escape from incest).

C — Hatred of Grandfather for Grandson: — Metastasio's "Cyrus;" the story of Amulius in the beginning of Titus Livius (motive, tyrannical avarice). Hatred of uncle for nephew: "The Death of Cansa," by Crichna Cavi. One of the facets of "Hamlet."

D — Hatred of Father-in-law for Son-in-law: — Alfieri's "Agis and Saul" (motive, tyrannical avarice). Historical example: Caesar and Pompey. Hatred of two

brothers-in-law, ex-rivals: "La Mer" (Jean Jullien, 1891)
— the only modern drama, I may note in passing, in
which one finds emotion increasing after the death of
the principal character. In this respect it conforms to
reality, in which we may experience shock or alarm, or
cry out in dread, but in which we do not weep, nor feel
sorrow to the full, until afterward, all hope being forever ended.

E — **Hatred of Mother-in-law for Daughter-in-law:**
— Corneille's "Rodogune" (motive, tyrannical avarice).

F — **Infanticide:** — "Conte de Noel" (Linant, 1899).
A part of the "Power of Darkness."

I will not repeat the list of degrees of relationship
into which this situation might be successively transferred. The case of hatred between sisters, one frequent
enough, will offer, — even after "Le Carnaval des Enfants" (de Bouhélier) — an excellent opportunity for a
study of feminine enmities, so lasting and so cruel;
hatred of mother and daughter, of brother and sister,
will be not less interesting; the same may be said for
the converse of each class which has furnished our examples. May there not be an especially fine dramatic
study in the deep subject, — heretofore so vulgar because treated by vulgar hands, — the antipathy of the
mother and the husband of a young woman? Does it
not represent the natural conflict between the ideal,
childhood, purity, on the one hand, and on the other
Life, vigorous and fertile, deceptive but irresistibly
alluring?

Next the motive of hatred, changing a little, may
vary from the everlasting "love of power" alleged in
nearly all extant examples, and, what is worse, invariably painted in the strained attitudes of neo-classicism.

The character of the common parent, torn by affection for both adversaries in these struggles, has been
little modified since the day when Aeschylus led forth,
from the tomb to which tradition had consigned her, his
majestic Jocaste. The rôles of two parents at enmity
could well be revived also. And I find no one but Beaumont and Fletcher who has drawn vigorously the insti-

gators of such impious struggles; characters whose in-famy is sufficient to be well worthy of attention, never-theless.

With the enmities of kinsmen are naturally connected the enmities which spring up between friends. This nuance will be found in the following situation.

FOURTEENTH SITUATION

RIVALRY of KINSMEN

(The Preferred Kinsman; the Rejected Kinsman; the Object)

This situation seems, at first glance, to present ten times the attraction of the preceding. Does not Love, as well as Jealousy, augment its effect? Here the charms of the Beloved shine amid the blood of battles fought for her sake. What startled hesitancies, what perplexities are hers; what fears of avowing a preference, lest pitiless rage be unchained!

Yes, the Beloved one, the "Object"—to use the philosophic name applied to her in the seventeenth century—will here be added to our list of characters. But . . . the Common Parent, even if he does not disappear, must lose the greater part of his importance; the Instigators will pale and vanish in the central radiance of the fair Object. Doubtless the "love scenes" will please, by their contrast to the violence of the play; but the dramatic purist may raise his brows, and find — perhaps — these turtle-dove interludes a trifle colorless when set in the crimson frame-work of fratricide.

Furthermore, there persists in the psychologist's mind the idea that Rivalry, in such a struggle, is no more than a pretext, the mask of a darker, more ancient hatred, a physiological antipathy, one might say, derived from the parents. Two brothers, two near relatives, do not proceed, on account of a woman, to kill each other, unless predisposed. Now, if we thus reduce the motive to a mere pretext, the Object at once pales and diminishes in importance, and we find ourselves returning to the Thirteenth Situation.

Is the Fourteenth, then, limited to but one class, a mere derivative of the preceding? No; it possesses, fortunately, some germs of savagery which permit of its development in several directions. Through them it may trend upon "Murderous Adultery," "Adultery Threatened," and especially upon "Crimes of Love" (incests, etc.). Its true form and value may be ascertained by throwing these new tendencies into relief.

A (1) — **Malicious Rivalry of a Brother:** — "Britannicus;" "Les Maucroix" by Delpit (the Common Parent here gives place to a pair of ex-rivals, who become almost the Instigators); "Boislaurier" (Richard, 1884). From fiction: "Pierre et Jean," by de Maupassant. Case in which rivalry is without hatred: "1812" (Nigond, 1910).

(2) — **Malicious Rivalry of Two B r o t h e r s:** — "Agathocle," "Don Pèdre," Adélaide du Guesclin" and "Amèlie," all by Voltaire, who dreamed of carving a kingdom all his own, from this sub-class of a single situation.

(3) — **Rivalry of Two Brothers, With Adultery on the Part of One:** — "Pelléas et Mélisande" by Maeterlinck.

(4) — **Rivalry of Sisters:** — "La Souris" (Pailleron, 1887); "L'Enchantment" (Bataille, 1900); "Le Demon du Foyer" (G. Sand). Of aunt and niece: "Le Risque" (Coolus, 1909).

B (1) — **Rivalry of Father and Son, for an Unmarried Woman:** — Metastasio's "Antigone;" "Les Fossiles" (F. de Curel); "La Massière" (Lemaitre, 1905); "La Dette" (Trarieux, 1909); "Papa" (de Flers and de Caillavet, 1911); Racine's "Mithridate," in which the rivalry is triple, between the father and each of the sons, and between the two sons. Partial example: the beginning of Dumas' "Père Prodigue."

(2) — **Rivalry of Father and Son, for a Married Woman:** — "Le Vieil Homme" (Porto-Riche, 1911).

(3) — Case Similar to the Two Foregoing, But in Which the Object is Already the Wife of the Father. (This goes beyond adultery, and tends to result in incest, but the purity of the passion preserves, for dramatic effect, a fine distinction between this sub-class and Situation XXVI) : — Euripides' "Phenix;" (a concubine is here the object of rivalry) ; Schiller's "Don Carlos;" Alfieri's "Philip II."

(4) — Rivalry of Mother and Daughter: — "L'Autre Danger" (Donnay, 1902).

C — Rivalry of Cousins: (which in reality falls into the following class) : — "The Two Noble Kinsmen," by Beaumont and Fletcher.

D — Rivalry of Friends: — Shakespeare's "Two Gentlemen of Verona;" "Aimer sans Savoir Qui" by Lope de Vega; Lessing's "Damon;" "Le Coeur a ses Raisons" (de Flers and de Caillavet, 1902) ; "Une Femme Passa" (Coolus, 1910).

FIFTEENTH SITUATION

MURDEROUS ADULTERY

(Elements: Two Adulterers; a Betrayed Husband or
Wife)

This, to my mind, is the only strongly appealing form
in which adultery can be presented; otherwise is it not
a mere species of housebreaking, the less heroic in that
the Object of theft is an accomplice, and that the house-
hold door, already thrown open by treachery, requires
not even a push of the shoulder? Whereas this treachery become at least logical and endurable in so far as
it is a genuinely sincere folly, impassioned enough to
prefer assassination to dissimulation and a base sharing
of love.

A (1) — **The Slaying of a Husband by, or for, a
Paramour:** — The "Agamemnons" of Aeschylus, of Seneca and of Alfieri; Webster's "Vittoria Corombona;"
"Pierre Pascal;" "Les Emigrants" (Hirsch, 1909);
"L'Impasse" (Fread Amy, 1909); "Partage de Midi"
(Paul Claudel); "Amour" (Leon Hennique, 1890); the
beginning of the "Power of Darkness." Historic example, with pride and shame as motives for the crime: the
legend of Gyges and Candaules. From fiction: the first
part of "Thérèse Raquin."

(2) — **The Slaying of a Trusting Lover:** — "Samson
et Dalila" (opera by Saint-Saëns, 1890).

B — **Slaying of a Wife for a Paramour, and in Self-**

Interest: — Seneca's "Octavia" and also Alfieri's; "La Lutte pour la Vie" by Daudet (in which cupidity dominates adultery); "The Schism of England" by Calderon; "Zobeide" by Gozzi. Narrative example: Bluebeard. Historic: the murder of Galeswinthe.

Hints for varying and modifying this situation: —

The betrayed husband or wife may be either more or less powerful, more or less sympathetic in character, than the slayer. The blindness of the intended victim may be more or less complete at various moments of the action; if it be dispelled, partly or fully, it may be by chance, by some imprudent act of the guilty ones, by a warning, etc.

Between the victim and the intruder, ties of affection, of duty, of gratitude, may have previously existed; ties very real to one or the other of the two. They may be relatives; they may find themselves united by some work or responsibility in common. The Victim, whether he be pursued openly or secretly, will be, doubtless, the object of an old rancor, either on the part of the consort or of the intruder; the origin of this rancor may be in any one of the imaginable offenses by which a human being is wounded in his family affections, his loves, his ideals, etc., or in his pride of birth, of name, of achievement; in his interests, (money, property, power, freedom); in any one of the external radiations of life.

Of the two adulterers, one may be but an instrument — impassioned or resigned, unconscious or involuntary — of the other, and may later be rejected, the end being attained; the blow may be struck by one of the two traitors alone, or it may be that neither of them has stained his own hands with the crime, which has been committed by a new character, perhaps unintentionally, or perhaps from love of one of the two Adulterers, who has utilized and directed this passion, or has let it move of its own accord toward the desired and criminal end.

A multitude of other characters will be, in varying degrees, the means employed, the obstacles, secondary victims, and accomplices in the sinister deed; the deed itself may be brought about according to the author's

choice among the numberless circumstances which the
Law has foreseen, with divers details such as court trials
suggest.

If a more complicated action is desired, interweave
(as Hennique has done) a rivalry of Kinsmen, an unnatural love (see Euripides' Chrysippe), an ambitious purpose and a conspiracy.

SIXTEENTH SITUATION

MADNESS

(Elements: Madman and Victim)

The origin of certain human actions lies hidden in fearful mystery; a mystery wherein the ancients believed they discerned the cruel smile of a god, and wherein our scientists, like the Chinese philosophers believe, they recognize the desires, prolonged and hereditary, of an ancestor. A startling awakening it is for Reason, when she finds on all sides her destiny strewn with corpses or with dishonors, which the Other, the unknown, has scattered at his pleasure. At this calamity, greater than death, how our kindred must weep and tremble; what terror and suspense must arise in their minds! And the victims, whose cries are lost in the mute heavens; the beloved ones pursued in unreasoning rage which they cannot comprehend! What variations of the inconscient are here: folly, possession, divine blindness, hypnosis, intoxication, forgetfulness!

A (1) — **Kinsmen Slain in Madness:** — "Athamas" and the "Weavers of Nets" by Aeschylus; "Hercules Furens" by Euripides and by Seneca; "Ion" by Euripides.

(2) — **A Lover Slain in Madness:** — "La Fille Eliza," by Edmond de Goncourt; "La Tentation de Vivre" (Louis Ernault). A lover on the point of slaying his mistress in madness: Example from fiction: "La Bête Humaine." Familiar instances: Jack the Ripper; the Spaniard of Montmartre, etc.

(3) — **Slaying or Injuring of a Person not Hated:** — "Monsieur Bute" (Biollay, 1890). Destruction of a work: "Hedda Gabler."

B — **Disgrace Brought Upon Oneself Through Madness:** — Aeschylus' "Thracians;" Sophocles' "Ajax;" to some extent "Saul" (Gide).

C — **Loss of Loved Ones Brought About by Madness:** — "Sakuntala" by Kalidasa (form, amnesia). The philtre of Hagen, in Wagner.

D — **Madness Brought on by Fear of Hereditary Insanity:** — "L'Etau" (André Sardou, 1909).

The case of A (3), transferred to the past and treated according to a quid-pro-quo process, is that of one of the merriest comedies of the nineteenth century, "L'Affaire de la rue de Lourcine" by Labiche.

Numberless examples of this Sixteenth Situation have filled the disquieting pages of alienists' journals. Mental diseases, manias of various types, offer powerful dramatic effects which have not yet been exploited. These furnish, doubtless, but points of departure toward the Situation whose real investiture takes place at the moment of the hero's restoration to reason, — which is to say, to suffering. But if it ever happens that these three phases — the etiology of delirium, its access, and the return to a normal condition — are treated with equal strength and vigor, what an admirable work will result!

The first of the three stages, which bears upon the explanations of insanity, has been variously held to be divine (by the Greeks), demoniac (by the Church), and, in our own times, hereditary and pathological. Hypnotism has recently created another nuance; the hypnotist here forms a substitute, — a sorry one, it is true, — for divinity or demon. Drunkenness furnishes us a nuance unfamiliar to Greece; what is today more commonplace, and at the same time more terrible, than the disclosure of an important secret or the committing of a criminal act, while under the influence of drink?

Is it necessary to say that all ties, all interests, all

human desires, may be represented crossed and illuminated by the light of dementia?

For the rest, this situation of Madness is far from having been neglected in our theater. Shakespeare, in his most personal dramas, has made use of insanity in the leading rôles. Lady Macbeth is a somnambulist and dies in hysteria, her husband is a victim of hallucinations; the same may be said of Hamlet, who is a lypemaniac besides; of Timon also; Othello is an epileptic and King Lear completely deranged. It is on this account that the great William is so dangerous a model (Goethe would not read him more than once a year). He has played, to some extent, the same rôle as Michael-Angelo, — he has exaggerated the springs of action to the farthest limits of reality, beyond which his disciples fall immediately into mere ridiculous affectation.

On the other hand, if we except the pretext of studying insanity in itself, which "Ajax" has furnished from Astydamus to Ennius, and from Ennius to Emperor Augustus, I find nothing "Shakespearean" in the drama of antiquity except "Orestes." All other characters are in the enjoyment of their senses, and do not thereby become any less pathetic. "Œdipus" alone shows, in default of abnormality in the hero's psychologic constitution, external events of an extraordinary character (a resource since so largely used by the Romanticists of 1830 and later). But the rest of the antique dramatic types are evolved in accordance with normal passions, and under objective conditions relatively common.

SEVENTEENTH SITUATION

FATAL IMPRUDENCE

(The Imprudent; the Victim or the Object Lost)

To which are sometimes added "The Counsellor," a person of wisdom, who opposes the imprudence, "The Instigator," wicked, selfish or thoughtless, and the usual string of Witnesses, secondary Victims, Instruments, and so forth.

A (1) — **Imprudence the Cause of One's Own Misfortune:** — Sophocles' "Eumele;" Euripides' "Phaeton" (here the Counsellor is blended with the Instrumental character, in which, bound by a too-hasty oath, he finds himself in Situation XXIII, A (2), — obliged to sacrifice a kinsman to keep a vow); "The Master Builder," by Ibsen. From comedy: "L'Indiscret" (See, 1903).

(2) — **Imprudence the Cause of One's Own Dishonor:** — "La Banque de l'Univers" (Grenet-Dancourt, 1886). From fiction: "L'Argent" by Zola. Historic: Ferdinand de Lesseps.

B (1) — **Curiosity the Cause of One's Own Misfortune:** — Aeschylus' "Semele." Historic examples (which rise to the Twentieth Situation, "Sacrifices to the Ideal"): the deaths of many scholars and scientists.

(2) — **Loss of the Possession of a Loved One, Through Curiosity:** — "Psyche" (borrowed from the account which La Fontaine drew from Apuleius, himself the debtor of Lucius of Patras, and dramatized by Corneille, Molière and Quinault); "Esclarmonde" (Massenet, 1889). Legendary example: Orpheus bringing back Eurydice. This nuance tends toward Situations

XXXII and XXXIII, "Mistaken Jealousy" and "Judicial Error."

C (1) — **Curiosity the Cause of Death or Misfortune to Others:** — Goethe's "Pandora" and also Voltaire's; "The Wild Duck" by Ibsen. Legendary example: Eve.

(2) — **Imprudence the Cause of a Relative's Death:** —"La Mère Meurtriere de son Enfant" (a fourteenth-century Miracle of Notre-Dame); "On ne Badine pas avec l'Amour" (de Musset); "Rénee Mauperin," by the Goncourts. Familiar instances: blunders in the care of sick persons. "Louise Leclerq," by Verlaine. The cause of another's misfortune: "Damaged Goods" (Brieux, 1905).

(3) — **Imprudence the Cause of a Lover's Death:** — "Samson" by Voltaire; "La Belle aux Cheveux d'Or" (Arnould, 1882).

(4) — **Credulity the Cause of Kinsmen's Deaths:** — "Pelias" by Sophocles and "The Peliades" by Euripides. From fiction (credulity the cause of misfortune to fellow-citizens): "Port-Tarascon."

Establish in each of the preceding sub-classes equivalents to those cases which are presented in single instances in one class only, and we have the following subjects: — By Imprudence (meaning imprudence pure and simple, unconnected with curiosity or credulity) to cause misfortune to others; to lose possession of a loved one (lover, wife or husband, friend, benefactor, protege, etc.) ; to cause the death of a relative (any degree of kinship may be chosen) ; to cause the death of a loved one. By Curiosity (unmixed with imprudence or credulity) to cause the dishonor of a relative (the various kinds of dishonor are numerous enough, touching as they do upon probity, upon courage, upon modesty, upon loyalty) ; to cause the dishonor of a loved one; to cause one's own dishonor. To cause these dishonors by pure Credulity (unmixed with imprudence or curiosity). An examination of the Twelfth Situation will give us a primary idea of the way in which Ruse may be used to gain this credulity. By Credulity also to cause one's own misfortune, or lose possession of a loved one, or cause misfortune to others, or cause the death of a loved one.

Let us now pass to the causes which may precipitate — as readily as curiosity, credulity, or pure imprudence — an overhanging catastrophe. These causes are: — the infraction of a prohibition or law previously made by a divinity; the deadly effect of the act upon him who commits it (an effect due to causes perhaps mechanical, perhaps biological, perhaps judicial, perhaps martial, etc.); the deadly consequences of the act for the kindred or the beloved of him who commits it; a sin previously committed, consciously or unconsciously, and which is about to be revealed and punished.

Besides curiosity and credulity, other motives may determine the imprudence; in "The Trachiniae," for instance, it is jealousy. The same rôle might be given to any one of the passions, the emotions, the desires, the needs, the tastes, the human weaknesses; — sleep, hunger, muscular activity, gluttony, lust, coquetry, childish simplicity. As to the final disaster, it may assume many aspects, since it may fall in turn upon physical, moral or social well-being, whether by the destruction of happiness or honor, of property or power.

In the present situation, the Instigator, — who nevertheless is not essential, — may become worthy of figuring even as the protagonist; such is the case of Medea in "Pelias." This is perhaps the most favorable aspect in which the "villain" can be presented; imagine, for instance, an Iago becoming the principal character of a play (as Satan is of the world)! The difficulty will be to find a sufficient motive for him; ambition (partly the case in Richard III) is not always a convincing one, because of its "a priori" way of proceeding; jealousy and vengeance seem a trifle sentimental for this demoniac figure; misanthropy is too philosophic and honorable; self-interest (the case of Pelias) is more appropriate. But envy, — envy, which in the presence of friendly solicitude feels but the more keenly the smart of its wounds, — envy studied in its dark and base endeavors, in the shame of defeat, in its cowardice, and ending finally in crime, — here, it seems to me, is the ideal motive.

EIGHTEENTH SITUATION

INVOLUNTARY CRIMES OF LOVE

(The Lover; the Beloved; the Revealer)

This and the following situation stand out as the most fantastic and improbable of all the silhouettes upon our dramatic horizon. Nevertheless they are, in themselves, quite admissible, and at least not rarer today than they were in heroic times, through adultery and prostitution, which never flourished more generally than at present. It is merely the disclosure which is less frequent. Yet many of us have seen certain marriages, apparently suitable, planned and arranged, as it were, by relatives or friends of the families, yet obstinately opposed, avoided and broken off by the parents, seemingly unreasonable, but in reality only too certain of the consanguinity of the lovers. Such revelations, then, still take place, although without their antique and startling éclat, thanks to modern custom and our prudent prudery.

Its reputation for fabulous monstrosity was in reality attached to our Eighteenth Situation by the unequalled celebrity of the theme of "Œdipus," which Sophocles treated in a style almost romantic, and which his imitators have ever since overloaded with fanciful arabesques more and more chimerical and extraordinary.

This situation and the following — as indeed to some extent all thirty-six — may be represented, as the author chooses, in one of two lights. In the first, the fatal error is revealed, simultaneously to the spectator and to the character, only after it is irreparable, as in Class A; and here the state of mind strongly recalls the Sixteenth. In the second, the spectator, informed of the truth, sees the character walk unconsciously toward the crime, as though in a sinister sort of blindman's-buff, as in Classes B, C and D.

A (1) — Discovery That One Has Married One's Mother: — The "Œdipus" of Aeschylus, of Sophocles, of Seneca, of Anguillara, of Corneille, of Voltaire, not to speak of those of Achaeus, Philocles, Melitus, Xenocles, Nicomachus, Carcinus, Diogenes, Theodecte, Julius Caesar; nor of those of Jean Prévost, Nicolas de Sainte-Marthe, Lamothe, Ducis, J. Chenier, etc. The greatest praise of Sophocles consists in the astonishment we feel that neither the many imitations, nor the too well-known legend of the abandonment on Cithaeron, nor the old familiar myth of the Sphinx, nor the difference in the ages of the wedded pair, — that none of these things has made his work appear unnatural or unconvincing.

(2) — Discovery That One Has Had a Sister as Mistress: — Tasso's "Torrismond;" "The Bride of Messina" by Schiller. This case, obviously a more frequent one, becomes unconvincing in the latter drama, when combined with the Nineteenth Situation. Example from fiction: "L'Enfant Naturel," by Sue.

B (1) — Discovery That One Has Married One's Sister: — "Le Mariage d' André" (Lemaire and de Rouvre, 1882). This being a comedy, the error is discovered in time to be remedied, and the play "ends happily." "Abufar" by Ducis, which also falls under a preceding classification.

(2) — The Same Case, in Which the Crime Has Been Villainously Planned by a Third Person: — "Heraclius" (this gives, despite its genius, rather the feeling of a nightmare than of a terrible reality).

(3) — Being Upon the Point of Taking a Sister, Unknowingly, as Mistress: — Ibsen's "Ghosts." The mother, a knowing witness, hesitates to reveal the danger, for fear of subjecting the son to a fatal shock.

C — Being Upon the Point of Violating, Unknowingly, a Daughter: — Partial example: "La Dame aux Domino Rose" (Bouvier, 1882).

D (1) — **Being Upon the Point of Committing an Adultery Unknowingly** (the only cases I have found in all drama): — "Le Roi Cerf" and "L'Amour des Trois Oranges," both by Gozzi.

(2) — **Adultery Committed Unknowingly:** — P r o b-ably the "Alcmene" of Aeschylus; "Le Bon Roi Dago-bert" (Rivoire, 1908). From fiction: the end of "The Titan," by Jean-Paul Richter.

The various modifications of incest and other forbid-den loves, which will be found in Situation XXVI, may be adapted in the same manner as those here classified.

We have seen above instances of adultery committed through a mistake on the part of the wife; it might also be through a mistake by the husband. This error is es-pecially likely to be made by that one of the two adult-erers who is unmarried; what is more common, for ex-ample, in the life of "pleasure," than to discover — a little tardily — that one's mistress is a married woman?

Ignorance of the sex of the beloved is the point upon which "Mademoiselle de Maupin" turns; there is in the first place a mistake (comedy), upon which are built the obsidional struggles of a soul (tragi-comedy), from which there finally results, when the truth is disclosed, a brief tragic dénouement.

NINETEENTH SITUATION

SLAYING OF A KINSMAN UNRECOGNIZED

(The Slayer; the Unrecognized Victim)

Whereas the Eighteenth Situation attains its highest degree of emotion after the accomplishment of the act, (doubtless because all the persons concerned in it survive, and the horror of it lies chiefly in the consequences), the Nineteenth, on the contrary, in which a victim is to perish and in which the interest increases by reason of the blind premeditation, becomes more pathetic in the preparations for the crime than in the results. This permits a happy ending, without the necessity of recourse, as in the Eighteenth, to a comedy-process of error. A simple recognition of one character by another will suffice, — of which our Situation XIX is, in effect, but a development.

A (1) — **Being Upon the Point of Slaying a Daughter Unknowingly, by Command of a Divinity or an Oracle:** — Metastasio's "Demophon." The ignorance of the kinship springs from a substitution of infants; the interpretation of the oracle's words is erroneous; the "jeune première," at one point in the action, believes herself the sister of her fiancé. This linking of three or four mistakes (unknown kinship, in the special light of the situation we are now studying, a supposed danger of incest, as in B (2) of the preceding, and finally a misleading ambiguity of words, as in the majority of comedies) suffices to constitute what is called "stirring" action, characteristic of the intrigues brought back into vogue by the Second Empire, and over whose intricate entanglements our chroniclers waxed so naively enthusiastic.

(2) — Through Political Necessity: — "Les Guèbres" and "Les Lois de Minos" by Voltaire.

(3) — Through a Rivalry in Love: — "La Petite Mionne" (Richebourg, 1890).

(4) — Through Hatred of the Lover of the Unrecognized Daughter: — "LeRoi s'amuse" (in which the discovery takes place after the slaying).

B (1) — Being Upon the Point of Killing a Son Unknowingly: — The "Telephus" of Aeschylus and of Sophocles (with incest as the alternative of this crime); Euripides' "Cresphontes;" the "Meropes" of Maffei, of Voltaire and of Alfieri; Sophocles' "Creusa;" Euripides' "Ion." In Metastasio's "Olympiad" this subject is complicated by a "Rivalry of Friends." A Son Slain Without Being Recognized: — Partial example: the third act of "Lucrèce Borgia;" "The 24th of February," by Werner.

(2) — The Same Case as B (1), Strengthened by Machiavellian Instigations: — Sophocles' "E u r y a l e;" Euripides' "Ægeus."

(3) — The Same Case as B (2), Intermixed With Hatred of Kinsmen (that of grandfather for grandson): — Metastasio's "Cyrus."

C — Being Upon the Point of Slaying a Brother Unknowingly: (1) — Brothers Slaying in Anger: — The "Alexanders" of Sophocles and of Euripides. (2) — A Sister Slaying Through Professional Duty: — "The Priestesses" of Aeschylus; "Iphigenia in Tauris," by Euripides and by Goethe, and that projected by Racine.

D — Slaying of a Mother Unrecognized: — Voltaire's "Semiramis;" a partial example: the dénouement of "Lucrèce Borgia."

E — A Father Slain Unknowingly, Through Machiavellian Advice: (see XVII): — Sophocles' "Pelias" and Euripides' "Peliades;" Voltaire's "Mahomet" (in which the hero is also upon the point of marrying his sister unknowingly). **The Simple Slaying of a Father Unrecognized:** — Legendary example: Laius. From romance: "The Legend of Saint Julian the Hospitaller." **The Same Case Reduced From Murder to Simple Insult:** — "Le Pain d'Autrui" (after Turgenieff, by Ephraim and Schutz, 1890). **Being Upon the Point of Slaying a Father Unknowingly:** — "Israel" (Bernstein, 1908).

F (1) — **A Grandfather Slain Unknowingly, in Vengeance and Through Instigation:** — "Les Burgraves" (Hugo).

(2) — **Slain Involuntarily:** — A e s c h y l u s' "Polydectes."

(3) — **A Father-in-Law K i l l e d Involuntarily:** — Sophocles' "Amphitryon."

G (1) — **Involuntary Killing of a Loved Woman:** — Sophocles' "Procris." Epic example: Tancred and Clorinda, in "Jerusalem Delivered." Legendary example (with change of the sex of the person loved): Hyacinthus.

(2) — **Being Upon the Point of Killing a Lover Unrecognized:** — "The Blue Monster" by Gozzi.

(3) — **Failure to Rescue an Unrecognized Son:** — "Saint Alexis" (a XIV Century Miracle of Notre-Dame;) "La Voix du Sang" (Rachilde).

Remarkable is the liking of Hugo (and consequently of his imitators) for this somewhat rare situation. Each of the ten dramas of the old Romanticist contains it; in two of them, "Hernani" and "Torquemada," it is in a manner accessory to the Seventeenth (Imprudence) fatal to the hero also; in four ("Marion Delorme," "Angelo," "La Esmerelda," "Ruy Blas") this case of involuntary injury to a loved one supplies all the action and furnishes the best episodes; in four others ("Le Roi s'amuse," "Marie Tudor," "Lucrèce Borgia," "Les Burgraves") it serves furthermore as dénouement. It would seem, indeed, that drama, for Hugo, consists in this: the causing, directly or indirectly, of the death of a loved one; and, in the work wherein he has accumulated the greatest number of theatrical effects — in "Lucrèce Borgia" — we see the same situation returning no less than five times. Near the first part of Act I, Gennaro permits his unrecognized mother to be insulted; in the second part, he himself insults her, not knowing her for his mother; in Act II she demands and is granted, the death of her unrecognized son, then finds she has no recourse but to kill him herself, then is again insulted by him; finally, in Act III, she poisons him, and, still unknown, is insulted, threatened and slain by him.

Be it noted that Shakespeare has not in a single instance employed this Nineteenth Situation, an altogether accidental one, having no bearing upon his powerful studies of the will.

TWENTIETH SITUATION

SELF-SACRIFICING FOR AN IDEAL

(The Hero; the Ideal; the "Creditor" or the Person or
Thing Sacrificed)

The four themes of Immolation, of which this is the
first, bring before us three corteges: — Gods (XX and
XXIII), Kindred (XXI and XXIII), and Desires
(XXII). The field of conflict is no longer the visible
world, but the Soul.

Of these four subjects, none is nobler than this of our
Twentieth Situation, — all for an ideal! What the ideal
may be, whether political or religious, whether it be
called Honor or Piety, is of little importance. It exacts
the sacrifice of all ties, of interest, passion, life itself, —
far better, however, under one of the three following
forms, if it be tarnished with the slightest, even although
the most sublime, egoism.

A (1) — **Sacrifice of Life for the Sake of One's
Word:** — The "Regulus" of Pradon and also of Metastasio; the end of "Hernani" (Carthage and Don Ruy
Gomez are the "Creditors"). Is it not surprising that a
greater number of examples do not at once present
themselves to us? This fatality, the work of the victim
himself, and in which the victory is won over Self, — is
it not worthy to illuminate the stage with its sacrificial
flames? There is, nevertheless, no necessity for choos-
ing a hero of an almost too-perfect type, such as Regulus.

(2) — **Life Sacrificed for the Success of One's People:** — "The Waiting-Women" by Aeschylus; "Protesi-
las" by Euripides; "Themistocles" by Metastasio. Partial examples: "Iphigenia in Aulis," by Euripides and by

Racine. Historic examples: Cordus; Curtius; Latour d'Auvergne. **For the Happiness of One's People:** — The "Suffering Christ" of St. Gregory Nazianzen.

(3) — **Life Sacrificed in Filial Piety:** — "The Phoenician Women" by Aeschylus; the "Antigones" of Sophocles and Euripides; of Alamanni and Alfieri.

(4) — **Life Sacrificed for the Sake of One's Faith:** — "The Miracle of St. Ignace of Antioch" (XIV Century); "Vive le Roi" (Han Rymer, 1911); "Cesar Birotteau" (Fabre, after Balzac, 1911); "The Constant Prince" by Calderon; "Luther" by Werner. Familiar instances: all martyrs, whether to religion or science. In fiction: "L'Œuvre" by Zola. **For the Sake of One's King:** — "L'Enfant du Temple" (de Pohles).

B (1) — **Both Love and Life Sacrificed for One's Faith:** — "Polyeucte." In fiction "L'Evangeliste" (sacrifice of family and future for one's faith).

(2) — **Both Love and Life Sacrificed to a Cause:** — "Les Fils de Jahel" (Mme. Armand, 1886).

(3) — **Love Sacrificed to Interests of State:** — This is the favorite motif of Corneille, as in "Othon," "Sertorius," "Sophonisbe," "Pulcherie," "Tite et Bérénice." Add to these the "Bérénice" of Racine and the "Sophonisbe" of Trissino, that of Alfieri and that of Mairet; Metastasio's "Achilles in Scyro" and his "Dido;" Berlioz' "Troyons" (the best tragedy of his century); "L'Impératrice" (Mendes). The "Creditor" in this sub-class, remaining abstract, is easily confounded with the Ideal and the Hero; the "Persons Sacrificed," on the contrary, become visible; these are Plautine, Viriate, Syphax and Massinisse, Bérénice, Déidamie. In comedy: "S. A. R." (Chancel, 1908).

C — **Sacrifice of Well-Being to Duty:** — "Resurrection" by Tolstoi; "L'Apprentie" (Geffroy, 1908).

D — **The Ideal of "Honor" Sacrificed to the Ideal of "Faith":** — Two powerful examples, which for secondary reasons did not attain success (because the public ear was incapable of perceiving a harmony pitched so high in the scale of sentiment): "Theodore" by Corneille and "The Virgin Martyr" by Massinger. Partial example: the good hermit Abraham in Hroswitha.

TWENTY-FIRST SITUATION

SELF-SACRIFICE FOR KINDRED

(The Hero; the Kinsman; the "Creditor" or
the Person or Thing Sacrificed)

A (1) — **Life Sacrificed for that of a Relative or a
Loved One:** — The "Alcestes" of Sophocles, of Eurip-
ides, of Buchanan, of Hardy, of Racine (projected) of
Quinault, of Lagrange-Chancel, of Boissy, of Coypel, of
Saint-Foix, of Dorat, of Gluck, of H. Lucas, of Vau-
zelles, etc.

(2) — **Life Sacrificed for the Happiness of a Relative
or a Loved One:** — "L'Ancien" by Richepin. Two symmetrical works are "Smilis" (Aicard, 1884), in which the
husband sacrifices himself, and "Le Divorce de Sarah
Moore" (Rozier, Paton and Dumas fils), in which the
wife sacrifices herself. Examples from fiction and analogous to these two dramas are "Great Expectations" by
Dickens and "La Joie de Vivre" by Zola. Common examples: workmen in dangerous occupations.

B (1) — **Ambition Sacrificed for the Happiness of a
Parent:** — "Les Frères Zemganno" by Edmond de Goncourt. This ends with a dénouement the opposite of that
of "L'Œuvre."

(2) — **Ambition Sacrificed for the Life of a Parent:**
— "Madame de Maintenon" (Coppée, 1881).

C (1) — **Love Sacrificed for the Sake of a Parent's
Life:** — "Diana" by Augier; "Martyre" (Dennery, 1886).

(2) — **For the Happiness of One's Child:** — "Le
Reveil" (Hervieu, 1905); "La Fugitive" (Picard, 1911).

For the Happiness of a Loved One: — "Cyrano de Bergerac" by Rostand; "Le Droit au Bonheur" (C. Lemonnier, 1907).

(3) — The Same Sacrifice as 2, But Caused by Unjust Laws: — "La Loi de l'Homme" by Hervieu.

D (1) — Life and Honor Sacrificed for the Life of a Parent or Loved One: — "Le Petit Jacques." Case in which the loved one is guilty: "La Charbonnière" (Cremieux, 1884); "Le Frère d'Armes" (Garaud, 1887); "Le Chien de Garde" (Richepin, 1889). The Same Sacrifice Made for the Honor of a Loved One: — "Pierre Vaux" (Jonathan, 1882). A similar sacrifice, but of reputation only: "La Cornette" (Mlle. and M. Ferrier, 1909).

(2) — Modesty Sacrificed for the Life of a Relative or a Loved One: — Shakespeare's "Measure for Measure;" Euripides' "Andromache" and also Racine's; "Pertharite" by Corneille; "La Tosca" (Sardou, 1889). In fiction: "Le Huron" by Voltaire.

TWENTY-SECOND SITUATION

ALL SACRIFICED FOR A PASSION

(The Lover; the Object of the Fatal Passion;
the Person or Thing Sacrificed)

A (1) — **Religious Vows of Chastity Broken for a
Passion:** — "Jocelyn" by Godard. From fiction: "La
Faute de l'Abbe Mouret." In comedy: "Dhourtta
Narttaka."

(2) — **A Vow of Purity Broken:** — "Tannhauser."
Respect for a Priest Destroyed: — One aspect of "La
Conquête de Plassans."

(3) — **A Future Ruined by a Passion:** — "Manon" by
Massenet; "Sapho" by Daudet; "La Griffe" (Bernstein,
1906); the works of Louys in general.

(4) — **Power Ruined by Passion:** — Shakespeare's
"Antony and Cleopatra;" "Cléopâtre" by Sardou.

(5) — **Ruin of Mind, Health and Life:** — "La Glu"
(Richepin, 1883); "L'Arlesienne" (Daudet and Bizet);
"La Furie" (Bois, 1909). From fiction (see C): "Le
Possédé" by Lemmonnier. **Passion Gratified at the
Price of Life:** — "Une Nuit de Cléopâtre" (Gautier and
Masse).

(6) — **Ruin of Fortunes, Lives and Honors:** —
"Nana;" in part "La Route d'Emeraude" (Richepin,
after Demolder, 1909).

B — **Temptations (see XII) Destroying the Sense of
Duty, of Pity, etc.:** — "Salomé" (Oscar Wilde). From
fiction: "Herodias," and the attempts (repulsed) in "The
Temptation of Saint Anthony."

C (1) — **Destruction of Honor, Fortune and Life by Erotic Vice:** — "Germinie Lacerteux" by de Goncourt; "Rolande" (Gramont, 1888) ; "Maman Colibri" (Bataille, 1904). From fiction: "La Cousine Bette;" "Le Capitaine Burle."

(2) — **The Same Effect Produced by Any Other Vice:** — "Trente Ans ou la Vie d'un Joueur;" 'L'Assommoir." From fiction: "L'Opium" by Bonnetain; "Lelie" by Willy. In real life: our race-courses, our wine-shops, our cafes, our clubs, etc. In comedy: "Un Ange" (Capus, 1909).

Few situations, obviously, have received better and more constant treatment during our own century — to whose vices the Twenty-Second offers, in truth, a most appropriate mirror, in its amalgam of gloom and eroticism, at the same time presenting the most interesting studies of nervous pathology.

TWENTY-THIRD SITUATION

NECESSITY OF SACRIFICING LOVED ONES

(The Hero; the Beloved Victim; the Necessity for the Sacrifice)

Although similar to the three situations we have just considered, the Twenty-Third recalls, in one of its aspects, that destruction of natural affection which marked the Thirteenth, "Hatred of Kinsmen." The feelings which we here encounter in the protagonist are, it is true, of a nature altogether different. But through the intrusion of the element of Necessity, the end toward which he must proceed is precisely the same.

A (1) — **Necessity for Sacrificing a Daughter in the Public Interest:** — "The Iphigenias" of Aeschylus and of Sophocles; "Iphigenia in Aulis," by Euripides and by Racine; "Erechtheus" by Euripides.

(2) — **Duty of Sacrificing Her in Fulfillment of a Vow to God:** — The "Idoménées" of Crébillon, Lemierre, and Cienfuegos; the "Jepthes" of Buchanan and of Boyer. This nuance tends at first toward Situation XVII, "Imprudence," but the psychologic struggles soon give it a very different turn.

(3) — **Duty of Sacrificing Benefactors or Loved Ones to One's Faith:** — "Torquemada;" "Ninety-Three;" "Les Mouettes" (Paul Adam, 1906); "La Fille à Guillotin" (Fleischmann, 1910). Historic instances: Philip II; Abraham and Isaac.

B (1) — **Duty of Sacrificing One's Child, Unknown**

to Others, Under the Pressure of Necessity:—Euripides' "Melanippe;" "Lucrèce Borgia" (II, 5).

(2) — Duty of Sacrificing, Under the Same Circumstances, One's Father: — The "Hypsipyles" of Aeschylus, and of Metastasio; "The Lemnian Women" by
Sophocles.

(3) — Duty of Sacrificing, Under the Same Circumstances, One's Husband: — The "Danaides" of Phryn-
ichus, of Aeschylus, of Gombaud, of Salieri, of Spontini;
the "Lynceus" of Theodectes and of Abeille; the "Hy-
permnestres" of Metastasio, Riupeiroux, Lemierre, etc.

(4) — Duty of Sacrificing a Son-in-Law for the Public Good: — "Un Patriote" (Dartois, 1881). For the
Sake of Reputation: — "Guibor" (a XIV Century Miracle of Notre-Dame).

(5) — Duty of Contending with a Brother-in-Law for
the Public Good: — Corneille's "Horace," and that of
Arétin. The loyalty and affection subsisting between
the adversaries remove all resemblance to the Thirtieth.

(6) — Duty of Contending with a Friend: — "Jarnac"
(Hennique and Gravier, 1909).

Nuance B (B 1 for example) lends itself to a fine in-
terlacing of motifs. Melanippe finds herself (1st) forced
to slay her son, an order which she would have resisted
at the risk of her own life, but she is at the same time
(2nd) obliged to conceal her interest in the child for fear
of revealing his identity and thereby causing his certain
death. Similar dilemmas may be evolved with equal
success in all cases in which a character receives an in-
junction which he is unwilling to obey; it will suffice to
let him fall, by his refusal, into a second situation leading to a result equally repugnant or, better yet, identical.
This dilemma of action is again found in what is called
blackmail; we have also seen its cruel alternatives out-
lined in Class D of Situation XX ("Theodore," "The Virgin Martyr," etc.), and clearly manifested in Class D
(especially D 2) of Situation XXII ("Measure for Measure," "Le Huron," etc.) but it is there presented most
crudely, by a single character or event, of a nature tyrannical and odious. Whereas in "Melanippe" it results so

logically and pitilessly from the action that it does not occur to us to rebel against it; we accept it without question, so natural does it appear, so overwhelming.

Before leaving these four symmetrical situations, I would suggest a way of disposing their elements with a view to seeking states of mind and soul less familiar. We have just seen these forces marshalled: — Passion (vice, etc.); pure affection (for parents, friends, benefactors, and particularly devotion to their honor, their happiness, their interests); reasons of state (the success of a compatriot, of a cause, of a work); egoism (will to live, cupidity, ambition, avarice, vanity); honor (truthfulness, feminine chastity, promises to God, filial piety). Oppose these to each other, two by two, and study the ensuing conflicts.

The first cases produced will be those already cited. Here follow other and newer ones: — a passion or vice destroying interests of state (for in "Antony and Cleopatra" it is only the royal pomp of the two lovers which is impressive; one does not reflect upon the peril of their peoples); egoism (in the form of ambition, for example) struggling with faith in the soul of man, a frequent case in religious wars; egoism in this ambitious guise overcoming natural affection (the plotter denying or sacrificing his father, mother or friend offers a fine study); a conflict between personal honor and reasons of state (Judith in the arms of Holofernes; Bismarck falsifying the despatch of his master). Then oppose the various nuances to each other (the hero torn between his faith and the honor of his people, and so on). Subjects will spring up in myriads. (Special notice — the neo-classic tragedy having proved itself dead, — to psychological fiction, its legatee).

TWENTY-FOURTH SITUATION

RIVALRY OF SUPERIOR AND INFERIOR

(The Superior Rival; the Inferior Rival; the Object)

I would have preferred to make of this and the following (Adultery) a single situation. The difference lies in a contract or a ceremony, of variable importance according to the milieu, and which in any case does not materially change the dramatic emotions springing from the love contest; even this difference becomes quite imperceptible in polygamous societies (Hindu drama). Thus I would rather have created but one independent situation, of which the other should be a nuance. But I fear I should be accused of purposely compressing modern works into the smallest possible number of categories, for the two which we are now to analyze contain the major part of them.

We have already remarked that between "Hatred of Kinsmen" and "Rivalry of Kinsmen" the sole difference lies in the fact that in the latter there is embodied in human form the Object of dispute, the "casus belli." For the same reason we may bring together the situations "Rivalry of Superior and Inferior," "Adultery," and even "Murderous Adultery," and distinguish them from all the situations which portray struggle pure and simple (V, VII, VIII, IX, X, XI, XXX, XXXI). However, the beloved Object will more naturally appear in the present cases of sentimental rivalry than she could in the "Rivalry of Kinsmen," and nowhere does a more favorable opportunity present itself to the dramatic poet for portraying his ideals of love.

These cases are divided first according to sexes, then according to the degrees of difference in the rank of the rivals.

A — Masculine Rivalries (1) — Of a Mortal and an Immortal: — "Mrigancalckha" by Viswanatha; "Heaven and Earth" by Byron; "Polyphème" (Samain). **Of Two Divinities of Unequal Power:** — "Pandore" by Voltaire.

(2) — **Of a Magician and an Ordinary Man:** — "Tanis et Zelide," by Voltaire.

(3) — **Of Conqueror and Conquered:** — "Malati and Madhava" by Bhavabuti; "Le Tribut de Zamora" (Gounod, 1881); "LeSais" (Mme. Ollognier, 1881). **Of Victor and Vanquished:** — Voltaire's "Alzire." **Of a Master and a Banished Man:** — "Appius and Virginia" by Webster; "Hernani" and "Mangeront-Ils?" by Hugo; "Dante" (Godard, 1890). **Of Usurper and Subject:** — "Le Triumvirat" by Voltaire.

(4) — **Of Suzerain King and Vassal Kings:** — Corneille's "Attila."

(5) — **Of a King and a Noble:** — "The Earthen Toy-Cart" by Sudraka; "The Mill" and "Nina de Plata" by Lope; "Agésilas and Suréna" by Corneille; "Demetrius" by Metastasio; "Le Fils de Porthos" (Blavet, 1886).

(6) — **Of a Powerful Person and an Upstart:** — "Don Sanche" by Corneille; "La Marjolaine" (Richepin fils, 1907).

(7) — **Of Rich and Poor:** — "La Question d'Argent" by Dumas; "La Nuit de Saint-Jean" (Erckmann-Chatrian and Lacôme); "En Grève" (Hirsch, 1885); "Surcouf" (Planquette, 1887); "L'Attentat" (Capus and Descaves, 1906); "La Barricade" (Bourget, 1910); "La Petite Milliardaire" (Dumay and Forest, 1905). In fiction: part of "Toilers of the Sea." Relative inequality: "Mon Ami Teddy" (Rivoire and Besnard, 1910).

(8) — **Of an Honored Man and a Suspected One:** — "L'Obstacle" (Daudet, 1890); "Le Drapeau" (Moreau, 1879); "Devant l'Ennemi" (Charton, 1890); "Jack Tempête" (Elzear, 1882); "La Bucheronne" (C. Edmond,

1889). In comedy: "Le Mariage de Mlle. Boulemans" (Fonson and Wicheler, 1911).

(9) — **Rivalry of Two Who Are Almost Equal:** — "Dhourtta Samagana," the rivals here being master and disciple, as is also the case in "Maitres Chanteurs," but not in "Glatigny" (Mendes, 1906), nor in "Bohémos" (Zamacois, 1907).

(10) — **Rivalry of Equals, One of Whom Has in the Past Been Guilty of Adultery:** — "Chevalerie Rustique" (Verga, 1888).

(11) — **Of a Man Who is Loved and One Who Has Not the Right to Love:** — "La Esmerelda."

(12) — **Of the Two Successive Husbands of a Divorcée** — "Le Dédale" (Hervieu, 1903). By multiplying the number of husbands good comic effects might be secured.

B — **Feminine Rivalries, (1) — Of a Sorceress and an Ordinary Woman:** — "La Conquête de la Toison d'Or" by Corneille: "La Sorcière" (Sardou, 1903).

(2) — **Of Victor and Prisoner:** — "Le Comte d' Essex" by Thomas Corneille; the "Marie Stuart" of Schiller and also of Samson.

(3) — **Of Queen and Subject:** — "Marie Tudor" and "Amy Robsart" by Hugo; "Le Cor Fleuri" (Mikhael and Herold); "Varennes" (Lenôtre and Lavedan, 1904). The title of this sub-class is, it will be remembered, the only one cited of the so-called "Twenty-Four Situations" of Gérard de Nerval; we might indeed include under this denomination the examples of B 1, 2 and 4. But at most it can constitute only a half of one of the four classes of "Rivalry of Superior and Inferior," which itself has but the importance of one situation in a series of thirty-six.

(4) — **Of a Queen and a Slave:** — "Bajazet" by Racine; "Zulime;" part of "Une Nuit de Cléapâtre" (from Gautier, by V. Masse, 1885).

(5) — **Of Lady and Servant:** — "The Gardener's Dog" by Lope de Vega (wherein may be found what is perhaps the most successful of the many attempted portraits of an amorous "grande dame").

(6) — **Of a Lady and a Woman of Humbler Position:**

— "Francois-les-bas-bleus" (M e s s a g e r, 1883); "Le Friquet" (Willy and Gyp, 1904); "Petite Hollande" (S. Guitry, 1908); "L'Ane de Buridan" (de Fleurs and de Caillavet, 1909); "Trains de Luxe" (Hermant, 1909). **Of a Lady and Two Women of Humbler Class:** — "Les Passagères" (Coolus, 1906).

(7) — **Rivalry of Two Who Are Almost Equals, Complicated by the Abandonment of One** (this tends toward A (1) of Situation XXV): — Corneille's "Ariane;" "Benvenuto" (Diaz, 1890). In fiction: "La Joie de Vivre."

(8) — **Rivalry Between a Memory or an Ideal (That of a Superior Woman) and a Vassal of Her Own:** — "Semiramide Riconsciuta" by Metastasio; "Madame la Mort" by Rachilde (in which the field of struggle is subjective); "La Morte" by Barlatier; "L'Image" by Beaubourg. Symmetrical case in the masculine: "The Lady from the Sea," by Ibsen.

(9) — **Rivalry of Mortal and Immortal:** — "La Dame à la Faulx" (Saint-Pol Roux).

C — **Double Rivalry** (A loves B, who loves C, who loves D): — Metastasio's "Adrien;" Lessing's "Emilia Galotti;" "La Fermière" (d'Artois, 1889); "Ascanio" (Saint-Saens, 1890); "Les Deux Hommes" (Capus, 1908); "Le Circuit" (Feydeau and de Croisset, 1909); "L'Article 301" (Duval, 1909). It is permissible to extend the rivalry to three, four, etc., which will make it less commonplace, but will not greatly vary the effects, although sometimes the chain will end in a complete circle (that is to say, D will love A), or a partial one (D returning the love of C).

D — **Oriental Rivalries:** — We are beginning to take account of the fact that the divorce law was obtained chiefly through the efforts of our dramatic writers, less because they were convinced of its righteousness than because they felt the need of a renewal and increase of their limited combinations. They might, indeed, have breathed a fresher and purer air by turning toward Hindu polygamy! Goethe, Theophile Gautier (who foresaw the decadence of woman through the extension and increase of vice), Maurice Barrès ("L'Ennemi des Lois") seem to have felt something of the sort. We could wish that the misunderstandings of the modern home, in which archaic fidelity and genuine monogamy have almost ceased to exist, on one side especially, might be settled with a modicum of this spirit of tolerance.

(1) — **Rivalry of Two Immortals:** — "The Loves of Krishna" by Roupa.

(2) — **Of Two Mortals:** — "Agnimitra and Malavika," by Kalidasa.

(3) — **Of Two Lawful Wives:** — "The Necklace," by Sri Harshadeva; "The Statue" by Rajasekhara.

To the relative rank of the two rivals there is added, as a means of varying the theme, the position, with respect to them, of the beloved Object. The aspects of the struggle will depend, in fact, upon how near the prize may be to one of the adversaries, or how distant; upon whether the Object be of a rank inferior to both rivals, or midway between the two, or even superior to both.

TWENTY-FIFTH SITUATION

ADULTERY

(A Deceived Husband or Wife; Two Adulterers)

Without deserving to constitute a situation of itself alone, Adultery yet presents an interesting aspect of Theft (action from without) combined with Treason (action within). Schiller, following the example of Lope, was pleased to idealize brigandage; Hugo and the elder Dumas undertook for adultery a similar paradox; and, developing the process of antithesis by which were created "Triboulet" and "Lucrèce Borgia," they succeeded, once for all — and quite legitimately. The folly lies in the belief of the unthinking crowd in the excellence of the subject thus presented; in the public's admiration for the "Antonys" — but the public has ended by preferring the moving pictures to them.

First Case: — The author portrays the Adulterer, the stranger in the house, as much more agreeable, handsomer, more loving, bolder or stronger than the deceived husband. . . . Whatever arabesques may cover the simple and fundamental fact of Larceny, whatever complaisance may be shown by a tired public, there remains, nevertheless, beneath it all a basis of granite — the old-fashioned conscience; to it, the thing which is here vaunted is simply the breach of the Word of Honor of a contract — that word, that promise which was obeyed by the Homeric gods and by the knights of Chivalry no less than by ourselves; that base of every social agglomeration; that which savages and which convicts respect

81

between themselves; that primary source of order in the world of action and of thought. The spectators' attention may, of course, be momentarily turned from a point of view so strict, and quite naturally; through the heresies of the imagination almost anything may evoke a laugh. Do we not laugh heartily at the sight of a fat man tumbling ridiculously down a flight of steps, at the bottom of which he may break his neck? Anything likewise may evoke our pity; we have pity for the perjuries of the gambler and the drunkard, but it is mingled with contempt. Now, is it this sort of sad contempt which our dramatists wish to claim for their attractive young adulterers, as the reward of so much care and effort? If not, the effort has been a mistaken one.

Second Case: — The Adulterer is represented as less attractive and sympathetic than the unappreciated husband. This forms the sort of play known as "wholesome," which, as a matter of fact, is merely tiresome. A man whose pocketbook has been stolen does not on that account grow greater in our eyes, and when the information which he is in a position to furnish us is once obtained, our attention is turned from him and directed toward the thief. But if the latter, already far from heroic in his exploit, is in turn portrayed as still less interesting than his dupe, he merely disgusts us — and the adulterous wife appears but a fool to have preferred him. Then (with that childishness which most of us retain beneath our sophistication), scenting a foregone conclusion in the lesson which the author intends for us, and suspecting falsehood at the bottom of it, we grimace with irritation, disappointed to perceive, behind the story presented for our entertainment, the vinegarish smile of the school-teacher.

Third Case: — The deceived Husband or Wife is Avenged. Here, at last, something happens! But this vengeance, unfortunately, is merely one of the cases of the Third Situation.

Thus we shall not succeed with our Twenty-Fifth Situation except by treating it in a broadly human spirit, without dolefulness and without austerity. It will not be necessary to defend the thief nor the traitor, nor to take the part of their dupe. To comprehend them all, to have compassion upon all, to explain them all — which is to say to comprehend oneself, to have pity upon oneself, and to explain oneself — this is the real work to be accomplished.

A — A **Mistress Betrayed:** (1) — For a **Young Woman:** — S o p h o c l e s' "Women of Colchis;" the "Medeas" of Seneca and of Corneille; "Miss Sara Sampson" by Lessing; "Lucienne" (Gramont, 1890). These examples are, because of the final vengeance, symmetrical to the masculine of Class B.

(2) — **For a Young Wife** (the marriage preceding the opening of the play): — "Un Voyage de Noces" (Tiercelin, 1881).

(3) — **For a Girl:** — "La Veine" (Capus, 1901).

B — **A Wife Betrayed:** (1) — **For a Slave, Who Does Not Love in Return:** — "Maidens of Trachis" by Sophocles; "Hercules on Œta" by Seneca (the first part; as to the rest, see "Imprudence"); the "Andromache" of Euripides and that of Racine (in which this is one side of the drama; for the other, see "Sacrifices for Kinsmen").

(2) — **For Debauchery:** — "Numa Roumestan" by Daudet; "Francillon" by Dumas; "Serge Panine" by Ohnet; the opening part of "Mères Ennemies," which afterward turns to "Hatred of Kinsmen."

(3) — **For a Married Woman** (a double adultery): — "La Princesse Georges" and "L'Etrangére" by Dumas; "Monsieur de Morat" (Tarbe, 1887); "Les Menages de Paris" (Raymond, 1886); "Le Depute Leveau" (Lemaitre).

(4) — **With the Intention of B i g a m y:** — The "Almæons" of Sophocles and of Euripides.

(5) — **For a Young Girl, Who Does Not Love in Return:** — Shakespeare's "Henry VIII," and that of Saint-Saens; Alfieri's "Rosamonde" (a combination of the present and the preceding situations, for it is also a simple Rivalry of King and Subject).

(6) — **A Wife Envied by a Young Girl Who is in**

Love with Her Husband: — "Stella" by Goethe; "Dernier Amour" (Ohnet, 1890).

(7) — By a Courtesan: — "Miss Fanfare" (Ganderax, 1881, see B 2); "Proserpine" (Vacquerie and Saint-Saens, 1887); "La Comtesse Fredegonde" (Amigues, 1887); "Myrane" (Bergeat, 1890).

(8) — Rivalry Between a Lawful Wife Who is Antipathetic and a Mistress Who is Congenial: — "C'est la Loi" (Cliquet, 1882); "Les Affranchis" (Madame Lenéru, 1911).

(9) — Between a Generous Wife and an Impassioned Girl: — "La Vierge Folle" (Bataille, 1910); "La Femme de Demain" (Arthur Lefebvre, 1909).

C (1) — An Antagonistic Husband Sacrificed for a Congenial Lover: — "Angelo;" "Le Nouveau Monde" by Villiers de l'Isle Adam; "Un Drôle" (Yves Guyot, 1889); "Le Mari" (Nus and Arnould, 1889); "Les Tenailles" (Hervieu); "Le Torrent" (Donnay); "Decadence" (Guinon, 1901); "Page Blanche" (Devore, 1909).

(2) — A Husband, Believed to be Lost, Forgotten for a Rival: — "Rhadamiste et Zénobie" by Crébillon; "Jacques Damour" by Zola. The "Zénobie" of Metastasio, by the faithful love retained for her husband, forms a case unique (!) among the innumerable dramas upon adulterous passions. Compare "Le Dédale" (see XXIV, A 12).

(3) — A Commonplace Husband Sacrificed for a Sympathetic Lover: — "Diane de Lys" by Dumas; "Tristan and Isolde" by Wagner (with the addition of "Madness," produced by a love-potion); "Françoise de Rimini" (A. Thomas, 1882); "La Sérénade" (Jean Jullien, 1887); "L'Age Critique" (Byl, 1890); "Antoinette Sabrier" (Coolus, 1903); "La Montansier" (Jeofrin, de Flers and de Caillavet, 1904); "Connais-toi" (Hervieu, 1909). The same case without adultery: "Sigurd" (Reyer, 1885); "La Comtesse Sarah" (1886).

(4) — A Good Husband Betrayed for an Inferior Rival: — "L'Aveu" (Sarah Bernhard, 1888); "Révoltée" (Lemaître, 1889); "La Maison des Deux Barbeaux" (Theuriet, 1885); "André del Sarte" (Alfred de Musset);

"La Petite Paroisse" (Daudet, 1911); "Le Mannequin d'Osier" (France, 1904); "La Rencontre" (Berton, 1909). Cases of preference without adultery: "Smilis" by Aicard; "Les Jacobines" by Hermant (1907).

(5) — **For a Grotesque Rival:** — "The Fatal Dowry" by Massinger.

(6) — **For an Odious Rival:** — "Gerfaut" (from C. de Bernard, by Moreau, 1886); "Cœeur a Cœeur" (Coolus, 1907).

(7) — **For a Commonplace Rival, By a Perverse Wife:** — "La Femme de Claude" by Dumas; "Pot-Bouille" by Zola; "Rivoli" (Fauchois, 1911); "Les Male-filâtre" (Porto-Riche, 1904); "Soeurette" (Borteau-Loti). In fiction: "Madame Bovary."

(8) — **For a Rival Less Handsome, but Useful** (with comic false suspicions; that is, suspicions afterward thought to have been false): — "L'Echéance" (Jean Jullien, 1889).

D (1) — **Vengeance of a Deceived Husband** (dramas built upon a crescendo of suspicion): — "The Physician of His Own Honor" and "Secret Vengeance for Secret Outrage" by Calderon; "L'Affaire Clemenceau" by Dumas; "The Kreutzer Sonata" (after Tolstoi, 1910); "La Legende du Cœur" (Aicard, 1903); "Paraitre" (Donnay, 1906); "Les Miroirs" (Roinarrd); "The Enigma" by Hervieu (which borrows something from Situation XI of this name. A vengeance purely moral: "Après Moi" Bernstein, 1911); financial: "Samson," by the same author, (1907).

(2) — **Jealousy Sacrificed for the Sake of a Cause:** (tending toward "Sacrifices for an Ideal"): — "Les Jacobites" (Coppée, 1885); "Patrie" (Paladilhe, 1886). **Sacrificed Out of Pity:** — "La Famille d'Armelles" (Marras, 1883).

E — **A Husband Persecuted by a Rejected Rival:** — "Raoul de Crequi" (Delayrac, 1889). This case is symmetrical to B 7, and both proceed in the direction of "Murderous Adultery."

TWENTY-SIXTH SITUATION

CRIMES OF LOVE

(The Lover; the Beloved)

This is the only tragic situation of all those built upon Love, that subject being one essentially belonging to comedy (see XXVIII and XXIX).

Eight species of erotic crimes may be pointed out: —

First: Onanism, that "solitary vice" which does not lead to action, can furnish only melancholy silhouettes such as the legend of Narcissus and "Charlot s'amuse," or certain grotesqueries of Aristophanes, unless it be made the basis for a study of the weakening and collapse of the Will, in which case it might be grouped with drunkenness, gambling, etc., in Situation XXII.

Second: Violation, like murder, is but an act, generally a brief one and not a situation; at most it approaches "Abduction." Even the consequences to the perpetrator, like those of the

Third: Prostitution and its succeedant gallantry and Juanism (repetition of acts), do not become dramatic unless pursued by punishment, in which case they belong to the Fifth Situation. Nevertheless, if impunity be secured, the taste for violation and for prostitution tends toward the Twenty-Second.

Fourth: Adultery, whose character of theft has given rise to special situations already studied.

Fifth: Incest is divided in two principal directions. It may be committed in an ascendant-descendant line, in which case it implies either filial impiety or an abuse of authority analogous to that which we shall find in the Eighth variety of criminal love. It may also occur upon what may be called a horizontal line; that is, between consanguines or persons related by marriage.

A (1) — **A Mother in Love with Her Son:** — "Semiramis" by Manfredi, and by Crébillon; to explain and extenuate this case, the latter author has first used the Eighteenth (Involuntary Crimes of Love); "Les Cuirs de Boeuf" (Polti, 1898). Inverse case: "Le Petit Ami" by Leautaud.

(2) — **A Daughter in Love with Her Father:** — Alfieri's "Myrrha," whose psychology is drawn from that of "Phèdre."

(3) — **Violation of a Daughter by a Father:** — "The Cenci" by Shelley; the story of the Peau d'âne (intention only).

B (1) — **A Woman Enamored of Her Stepson:** — "Iobates" and "Phaedra" by Sophocles; the "Hippolytus" of Euripides and of Seneca; "Phèdre" by Racine. In comedy: "Madame l'Amirale" (Mars and Lyon, 1911). In almost none of the foregoing cases, it will be observed, is there a reciprocity of desire, whereas the passion, heretofore solitary, is shared, and the crime, unconscious at least on one side in "Myrrha," is boldly committed in

(2) — **A Woman and Her Stepson Enamored of Each Other:** — Zola's "Reneè" (drawn from his story "Curée") and similar to the quasi-incestuous passion of "Dr. Pascal." The love is platonic in Alfieri's "Philip II," and Schiller's "Don Carlos."

(3) — **A Woman Being the Mistress, at the Same Time, of a Father and Son, Both of Whom Accept the Situation:** — "L'Ecole des Veufs" (Ancey, 1889).

C (1) — **A Man Becomes the Lover of His Sister-in-Law:** — "La Sang-Brulé" (Bouvier, 1885); "Le Conscience de l'Enfant" (Devore, 1889). **The Man Alone Enamored:** — "Le Sculpteur de Masques" (Cromelynck, 1911).

(2) — **A Brother and Sister in Love with Each Other:** — Euripides' "Æolus;" "Canace" by Speroni;

" 'Tis Pity She's a Whore," Ford's masterpiece; "La Città Morta" by d'Annunzio.

Even after these works, there remains much more than a gleaning; an ample harvest is still before us. We may extend Class A to include the complicity of both parties (Nero and Agrippina furnish an example, according to Suetonius) ; a similar example, although fragmentary, exists for A 2, in the beginning of Shakespeare's "Pericles." B 1 may be reversed, the stepson's passion being unrequited by his father's wife, a case which is certainly not uncommon. We may also suppress the complicity in B 3, in C 1, and in C 2, allowing the infatuation to subsist upon one side only. Without going so far as the criminal act, a study of mere temptations or desires, well or ill controlled, has furnished subtile chapters in the psychologies of Seventeenth Century grande dames, such as Victor Cousin took delight in.

Finally, we may interlace the threads of each of these species of incest with one of the seven other classes of Crimes of Love; under the form of ignorance, the fifth and sixth classes are mingled in one of the episodes of "Daphnis and Chloe." Add the usual incidental rivalries. adulteries, murders, etc.

Sixth: Homosexuality in its two senses, the branches of pederasty and tribadism:

D (1) — A Man Enamored of Another Man, Who Yields: — Example from fiction: "Vautrin." Dramatic examples: the "Laius" of Aeschylus; the "Chrysippus" of Euripides. The latter tragedy appears to have been one of the finest, and perhaps the most moving, of all antiquity. Three situations were there superposed with rare success. Laius having conceived a passion, unnatural and, furthermore, adulterous, for the young Chrysippus, an epithalamium as terrible as that of Ford must have resulted, for here appeared and spoke the first man who had ever experienced such desires and dared to express and gratify them, and in his words lay the explanation of the wavering and fall of Chrysippus. Then followed the most indignant and pitiless jealousy on the part of Jocaste, wife of Laius. Against Chrysippus she roused the old envy of the young man's two brothers, an envy of the same type as that which armed the sons of Jacob against Joseph, but an envy which shows itself strangely menacing at the mere announcement of the names of these two brothers, — Atreus and Thyestes! The fratricide is accomplished, to the fierce joy of the queen; Laius learns the details from the lips of the dying Chrysippus himself. And, in some prediction — doubtless that of Tiresias, young at the time and not yet deprived of sight — there dawns the destiny of the two great families of tragedy par excellence, the Labdacides and the Atrides, beginning in these crimes and running through all Greek legend.

The tribadic or sapphic branch has not been used upon the stage; Mourey alone has attempted it, but in vain in his "Lawn Tennis." The objection which might be urged against it (and which probably explains why the drama, in the ages of its liberty, has made no use of it) is that this vice has not the horrible grandeur of its congener. Weak and colorless, the last evil habit of worn-out or unattractive women, it does not offer to the tragic poet that madness, brutal and preposterous, but springing from wild youth and strength, which we find in the criminal passion of the heroic ages.

Seventh: Bestiality, or passion for a creature outside the human species. Classed in general as a vice, it is of no use theatrically. Nevertheless, in

E — A Woman Enamored of a Bull: — "The Cretans" of Euripides seems to have revealed the emotions, after all conceivable, of this "Ultima Thule" of sexual perversion. Better than anywhere else, evidently, the illogical and mysterious character of the life of the senses, the perversion of a normal instinct, and the feeling of fatalism which its victims communicate, could here be presented in sad and awful nudity.

Eighth: The Abuse of Minor Children borrows something from each of the seven preceding varieties. That such a subject — so modern, so English — may in skillful hands become most pathetic, is readily apparent to those of us who read, a few years ago, the "Pall Mall Gazette."

TWENTY-SEVENTH SITUATION

DISCOVERY OF THE DISHONOR OF A LOVED ONE

(The Discoverer; the Guilty One)

From this Situation there results, almost immediately, a psychologic struggle similar to that of the Twenty-Third "Sacrifice of Loved Ones," but without the attraction of a high Ideal; this is replaced, in the present action, by the lash of shame.

A (1) — **Discovery of a Mother's Shame:** — "Madame Caverlet" by Augier; "Odette" and "Georgette" by Sardou; "Madame X" (Bisson, 1908); "Mrs. Warren's Profession" (Bernard Shaw); "Les Quarts d'Heure." (second part; Guiches and Lavedan, 1888). This sad destruction of a child's deepest respect and reverence is colored, in these works, by the terrors of the mother, by her blushes, by her remorse before the consequences of the past; through this last point the action ends in the Thirty-Fourth (Remorse). It remains unconnected in the second part of the "Marquis de Priola" (Lavedan, 1901).

(2) — **Discovery of a Father's Shame:** — "Vieille Histoire" (Jean Jullien, 1891); the dénouement of "Pierre et Thérèse" (Prevost, 1909).

(3) — **Discovery of a Daughter's Dishonor:** — Part of "La Fille du Depute" (Morel, 1881); of "Les Affaires sont les Affaires" (Mirbeau, 1902); "L'Oreille Fendue" (Nepoty, 1908).

B (1) — **Discovery of a Dishonor in the Family of**

One's Fiancee: — "L'Absente" (Villemer, 1889). Refinements of romance, whose mild tragedy consists in retarding the signature of a contract, and which corresponds also to the pseudo-Situation XXX (Forbidden Loves). Something of their dullness has already emanated from A 1 and A 2.

(2) — **Discovery that One's Wife Has Been Violated Before Marriage:** — "Le Secret de Gilberte" (Massiac, 1890). **Since the Marriage:** — "Flore de Frileuse" by Bergerat, with comic dénouement thanks to a "quid-pro-quo."

(3) — **That She Has Previously Committed a Fault:** — "Le Prince Zilah" (Claretie, 1885); part of Dumas' "Denise." Common instances: Marriages through agencies.

(4) — **Discovery that One's Wife Has Formerly Been a Prostitute:** — "Lena" (Berton and Mme. van Velde, 1886). That one's mistress has been a prostitute: "Marion Delorme." The same situation, from the point of view of "Remorse" (XXXIV), is encountered in Zola's "Madeleine."

(5) — **Discovery of Dishonor on the Part of a Lover** (this also borders upon XXXIV) : — "Chamillac" (Feuillet, 1886) ; "Le Crocodile" (Sardou, 1886).

(6) — **Discovery that One's Mistress, Formerly a Prostitute, Has Returned to Her Old Life** (with extenuating circumstances): — "La Dame aux Camellias" (Dumas); "La Courtisane" (Arnyvelde, 1905); part of "Manon Lescaut." But for feminine cunning, would not this be the normal course of all "bonnes fortunes?"

(7) — **Discovery that One's Lover is a Scoundrel, or that One's Mistress is a Woman of Bad Character:** — "Monsieur Alphonse" by Dumas; "Mensonges" by Emile Michelet. Since (as Palice remarks) liaisons would last forever if they were never broken off, and since the two lovers, who certainly know each other well, always give as the reason of their rupture the title of the present sub-class, the conclusion is as easy to draw as it is unflattering to the human species. **The Same Discovery Concerning a So-Called King:** — "Sire" (Lavedan, 1909).

(8) — **The Same Discovery Concerning One's Wife:**
— "Le Mariage d'Olympe" by Augier.

C — **Discovery that One's Son is an Assassin:** —
"Werner" by Byron; "La Policière" (Montepin, 1889).
The surprise is intensified in cases of parricide. Nuance
C is capable of infinite development.

D — Might constitute a distinct situation; there is
not only the discovery, but the duty of imposing punishment as well. This situation might serve as an inter-
mediary between the Twenty-Third, "Duty of Sacrificing
Kinsmen," and the Twenty-Seventh, which we are now
studying, and which would thus end with Class C.

(1) — **Duty of Punishing a Son Who is a Traitor to
Country:** — The "Brutus" of Voltaire, and of Alfieri. **A
Brother Who is a Traitor to His Party:** — "Etudiants
Russes" by Gilkin.

(2) — **Duty of Punishing a Son Condemned Under a
Law Which the Father Has Made:** — "L'Inflexible"
(P a r o d i, 1884); "L e T r i b u n" (Bourget, 1910);
"L'Apôtre" (Loyson, 1911).

(3) — **Duty of Punishing a Son Believed to be
Guilty:** — "L'Régiment" (Mary, 1890); "L'As de Tréfle"
(Decourcelle, 1883). This approaches XXXIII (Judicial
Error).

(4) — **Duty of Sacrificing, to Fulfill a Vow of Tyran-
nicide, a Father Until Then Unknown.** This imprudent
vow carries us back, at one point, to the Seventeenth
(Imprudence), and at another point the striking of an
unknown parent recalls also the Nineteenth. — "Severo
Torelli" (Coppée, 1883).

(5) — **Duty of Punishing a Brother Who is an
Assassin:** — "Casse-Museau" (Marot, 1881). From this
situation the kinsman-judge escapes for a moment, only
to fall into D 3, from which he returns with resignation
to D 5.

(6) — **Duty of Punishing One's Mother to Avenge
One's Father:** — (Situation IV arrested prematurely):
— "Le Cœur de Se-hor" (Michaud d'Humiac). The
Fourth is less in evidence in "Simone" (Brieux, 1908).

TWENTY-EIGHTH SITUATION

OBSTACLES TO LOVE

(Two Lovers; an Obstacle)

A (1) — **Marriage Prevented by Inequality of Rank:**
— "Nitétis" and "The Chinese Hero" by Metastasio:
"Le Prince Soleil" (Vasseur, 1889); second act of "La
Vie Publique" (Fabre, 1901); "Ramuntcho" (Pierre Loti,
1908); "L'Emigré" (Bourget, 1908). This is the senti-
mental-philosophical Situation of a great number of
eighteenth century works ("Nanine," etc.), in which a
lord invariably falls in love with a peasant girl. In
George Sand, on the contrary, it is always a lady who is
in love with a man of inferior rank; a sort of literature
which at least has inspired many gallant adventures of
our own time. The addition of one more little obstacle
— the marriage bond — furnishes the pretext for the real
intrigue of "Ruy Blas."

(2) — **Inequality of Fortune an Impediment to Marriage:** — "Myrtille" and in part "Friend Fritz" by Erckmann-Chatrian; "L'Abbe Constantin" by Halevy; "La
Petite Amie" (Brieux, 1902); "La Plus Faible" (Prevost,
1904); "La Veuve Joyeuse" (Meilhac, Léon and Stein,
1909); "Le Danseur Inconnu" (Bernard, 1909); "La
Petite Chocolatière" (Gavault, 1909); "Primerose;" "Le
Rêve" (from Zola's story by Bruneau); in fiction: "Le
Bonheur des Dames" — to mention only the more es-
timable works, leaving aside the endless number of
trivial plays imitative of Scribe, and the Romances of
Poor Young Men, Dames Blanches, etc., which make

our ears ring with confusing additions and subtractions,
until the unexpected final multiplication — "deus ex
machina" — which suddenly equalizes the two terms of
the problem, the two fortunes of the lovers, with the
most admirably symmetrical alignment of parallel zeros
— preceded, oh joy! oh bliss! on one side as on the other,
by two identical figures!

It must, of course, be recognized that these social and
conventional inequalities are mere puerile details, and
that the lovers, if they have but a little courage and sincerity, will overcome them without difficulty; they can
do so by simply leaving behind them titles and money,
and in a new country, under other names, bravely beginning life again together. If, istead of such bagatelles,
we might only be sometimes shown the more serious
obstacles of inequality of ages, of characters, of tastes
— which are at the same time so much more common!

They are, indeed, so frequent that a general theory
might be established with regard to them. The first
love (twenty years) seeks in its object equality of rank
and superiority of age (this is a fact well known to
those who have studied the cases of girl-mothers); the
second love, and in general the second period of emotional life (thirty years), addresses itself, audacity having been acquired, to superiors in rank but equals in
age; finally, the third love, or in a more general way the
third epoch of sentimental life, inclines by preference to
those who are younger and socially inferior. Naturally,
subdivision is here possible.

B — **Marriage Prevented by Enemies and Contingent
Obtacles:** — "Sieba" (Manzotti, 1883); "Et Ma-Soeur?"
(Rabier, 1911); "Le Péché de Marthe" (Rochard, 1910);
all fairy-plays, since the "Zéim" of Gozzi. In fine, a sort
of steeplechase process adapts itself to this situation,
but the chase is not one in which several rival steeds
and riders engage; throughout its course but a single
couple enters upon it, 'to end at the shining goal with
the usual somersault.

C (1) — **Marriage Forbidden on Account of the
Young Woman's Previous Betrothal to Another:** — "Il

Re Pastore" by Metastasio; and other pieces without number. The lovers will die if separated, so they assure us. We see them make no preparations to do so, but the spectator is good enough to take their word for it; the ardors, the "braises" — to use the exact language of the "grand siècle" — and other nervous phenomena in hypochondriacs of this sort cannot but offer some interest — not, however, for long.

(2) — **The Same Case, Complicated by an Imaginary Marriage of the Beloved Object:** — "Les Bleus de l'Amour" (Coolus, 1911).

D (1) — **A Free Union Impeded by the Opposition of Relatives:** — "Le Divorce" (Bourget, 1908); "Les Lys" (Wolf and Leroux, 1908).

(2) — **Family Affection Disturbed by the Parents-in-Law:** — "Le Roman d'Elise" (Richard, 1885); "Le Poussin" (Guiraud, 1908).

E — **By the Incompatibility of T e m p e r o f t h e Lovers:** — "M o n t m a r t r e" (Frondaie, 1911). "Les Angles du Divorce" (Biollay) belongs both to E and to D 2.

F — **Love** — but enough of this! What are we doing, co-spectators in this hall, before this pretended situation? Upon the stage are our two young people, locked in close embraces or conventionally attitudinizing in purely theatrical poses. What is there in all this worth remaining for? Let us leave it . . . What, Madame, you straighten yourself in your chair and crane your neck in excitement over the gesticulations of the "jeune premier?" But his sweetheart there beside him — have you forgotten that it is she whom he desires, or are the two of them playing so badly, is their dialogue so little natural that you forget the story enacted and fondly imagine yourself listening to a monologue a declaration addressed to you alone? And Monsieur there, with mouth open, eyes starting from his head, following with avidity every movement of the actress's lithe figure! Quick, my good man, another will be before you! Be consistent, at least! Spring upon the stage, break the insipid dandy's bones, and take his place!

Sorry return to promiscuity, in our overheated halls like lupanars, which the clergy is not altogether unreasonable in condemning! Do people gather here simply to study amatory manifestations? In that case, why not freely open training schools for courtesans? Is it for the benefit of the sidewalk traffic, later in the evening, that the public is here being prepared?

O fresh and stormy winds of Dionysian drama! Aeschylus where art thou who wouldst have blushed to represent aught of amorous passion but its crimes and infamies? Do we not, even yet, perceive the heights to which rise those chaste pinnacles of modern art, "Macbeth" and "Athalie?"

But why disturb ourselves? Turning our eyes from these summits to the scene before us, we do not feel depression; indeed, wᷜ indulge in a hearty laugh. These characters here before us? Why, they are but puppets of comedy, nothing more. And the effort of their misguided authors to make them serious and tragic despite their nature has resulted in mere caricature. In more intelligent hands, have not the best of our dramas wherein love is important (but not of the first importance, as in this XXVIII) returned logically and naturally to an indulgence of smiles? "Le Cid," which is the classic type of this sort, is a tragi-comedy, and all the characters surrounding Romeo and Juliet are frankly comic.

Nevertheless, our blind dramaturgy, with continued obstinacy, still breathes forth its solemnities in this equivocal rhythm. Whether the piece treats of sociology, of politics, of religion, of questions of art, of the title to a succession, of the exploitation of mines, of the invention of a gun, of the discovery of a chemical product, of it matters not what — a love story it must have; there is no escape. Savants, revolutionists, poets, priests or generals present themselves to us only to fall immediately to love-making or match-making. It becomes a mania. And we are asked to take these tiresome repetitions seriously!

This, then, is the actual stage of today. In my opinion, de Chirac alone has shown himself its courageously logical son — although a rejected one, — society, like an aged coquette, reserving always some secret sins, and fearing nothing so much as nudity, which would destroy the legend of her imaginary wicked charms, veiled, she willingly lets it be supposed, under her hypocrisy.

How grotesque an aspect will our ithyphallic obsession present, once it is crystallized in history, when we shall finally have returned to antique common sense!

TWENTY-NINTH SITUATION

AN ENEMY LOVED

(The Beloved Enemy; the Lover; the Hater)

A — The Loved One Hated by Kinsmen of the Lover. The preceding Situation might very well be absorbed into this.

(1) — **The Lover Pursued by the Brothers of His Beloved:** — "The Duchess of Malfi" by Webster; "The Broken Heart" by Ford.

(2) — **The Lover Hated by the Family of His Beloved:** — "The Story of Yayati" by Roudradeva (with the characteristic color of these Hindu rivalries, wherein jealousy is hardly perceptible); "The Victory of Pradyoumna" by Samara Dikchita; Metastasio's "Cato;" "La Grande Marnière" (Ohnet, 1888).

(3) — **The Lover is the Son of a Man Hated by the Kinsmen of His Beloved:** — "La Taverne des Trabans" and "Les Rantzau" by Erckmann-Chatrian. In comic vein: "Dieu ou pas Dieu," a romance by Beaubourg.

(4) — **The Beloved is an Enemy of the Party of the Woman Who Loves Him:** — "Madhouranirouddha" by Vira, the contemporary of Corneille; "Les Scythes" by Voltaire; "Almanzor" by Heine; "Lakmé" by Delibes; "Les Carbonari" (Nô. 1882); "Madame Thérèse" by Erckmann-Chatrian; "Lydie" (Miral, 1882); "Les Amazones" (Mazel); "Les Oberle" (Bazin, 1905); "Les Noces Corinthiennes" (France); "l'Exode" (Fauchois, 1904).

B (1) — The Lover is the Slayer of the Father of His

Beloved: — "Le Cid" (and the opera drawn from it) ; "Olympie" by Voltaire.

(2) — **The Beloved is the Slayer of the Father of Her Lover:** — "Mademoiselle de Bressier" (Delpit, 1887).

(3) — **The Beloved is the Slayer of the Brother of Her Lover:** — "La Reine Fiammette" (Mendès, 1889).

(4) — **The Beloved is the Slayer of the Husband of the Woman Who Loves Him, But Who Has Previously Sworn to Avenge that Husband:** — "Irène" by Voltaire.

(5) — **The Same Case, Except that a Lover, Instead of a Husband, Has Been Slain:** — "Fédora" (Sardou, 1882).

(6) — **The Beloved is the Slayer of a Kinsman of the Woman Who Loves Him:** — "Romeo and Juliet," this situation being modified by that of "Abduction" (elopement), then, with triple effect by XXXVI, "Loss of Loved Ones;" the first time mistakenly, the second time simply and actually, the third time doubly and simultaneously to both the families of the principal characters; "l'Ancêtre" (Saint-Saens and Lassus) : "Fortune and Misfortune of a Name" and "His Own Gaoler" by Calderon.

(7) — **The Beloved is the Daughter of the Slayer of Her Lover's Father:** — "Le Crime de Jean Morel" (Samson, 1890) ; "La Marchande de Sourires" (Judith Gautier, 1888).

The chief emotional element thus remains the same as in the Fifth (Pursuit), and Love here serves especially to present the pursued man under various favorable lights which have a certain unity. She whom he loves here plays, to some small extent, the rôle of the Greek chorus. Suppress the love interest, replace it with any other tie, however weak, or even leave nothing in its place, and a play of the type of Situation V, with all its terrors, will still remain. Attempt, on the contrary, to curtail the other interest, the enmity — to soften the vengeance — and to substitute any other element of difference or leave their place unfilled, and what will remain of tragic emotion? Nothing.

We have, then, reason to conclude that love — an

excellent motif for comedy, better still for farce — sweet or poignant as it may be in stories read in solitude, of which we can fancy ourselves hero or heroine, love is not, in reality, tragic, despite the virtuosity which has sometimes succeeded in making it appear so, and despite the prevalent opinion of this age of erotomania, which is now approaching its end.

THIRTIETH SITUATION

AMBITION

(An Ambitious Person; a Thing Coveted; an
Adversary)

A highly intellectual type of action is here presented,
for which there is no antique model, and from which
mediocrity usually keeps a respectful distance.

A — **Ambition Watched and Guarded Against by a
Kinsman or a Patriot Friend:** (1) — **By a Brother:** —
"Timoleon" by Alfieri. Historic instance (comic, that is
to say, feigned), Lucien and Napoleon Bonaparte.

(2) — **By a Relative or Person Under Obligation:** —
"Julius Caesar" by Shakespeare, "La Mort de Caesar"
by Voltaire; "Brutus II" by Alfieri. In "La Mort de
Caesar" there is a reappearance of the Nineteenth (Slaying of a Kinsman Unrecognized), so strong was the desire to recall the works of antiquity!

(3) — **By Partisans:** — "Wallenstein" by Schiller;
"Cromwell" by Hugo; "Marius Vaincu" (Mortier, 1911).

B — **Rebellious Ambition (akin to VIII, A 1):** —
"Sir Thomas Wyat" by Webster; "Perkin Warbeck" by
Ford; "Catilina" by Voltaire; Cade's insurrection in the
second part of Shakespeare's "Henry IV."

C (1) — **Ambition and Covetousness Heaping Crime
Upon Crime:** — "Macbeth" and "Richard III;" "Ez-
zelino" (A. Mussato); part of the "Cinq Doigts de
Birouk" (Decourcelle, 1883); "La-Bête Féroce" (Jules
Mary and Emile Rochard, 1908); "La Vie Publique"

(Fabre, 1901). In comedy: "Ubu-roi" (Jarry). In fiction: "La Fortune des Rougon" (with criminality attenuated to simple want of dignity); "Son Excellence Eugéne" (sacrifice of morality); the story of Lucien de Rubempré; a case of greed: "La Terre."

(2) — Parricidal Ambition: — "Tullia" by Martelli.

Ambition, one of the most powerful of passions, if it be not indeed the passion par excellence will always affect the spectator strongly, for he feels and knows that, once awakened in a man, it will cease only with his death. And how many are the objects of its desire! Tyrannical power, high rank honors, fortune (by inheritance, marriage, robbery, etc.), the conservation of riches (avarice), glory (political, scientific, literary, inventive, artistic), celebrity, distinction.

We have seen in Class A the ties which may unite the ambitious one and his adversary and the Situations which may result from them (XIX, XXIII, XXIV).

Here is one way among many to intensify the fury of C: mingle with it the sincerity of a faith, of a conviction; such a combination is found in the case of the Spaniards in Peru and in Flanders, and in the case of our own "gentle and intellectual" race under the League and under the Terror; in the case of Calvin, and of the Inquisition.

THIRTY-FIRST SITUATION

CONFLICT WITH A GOD

(A Mortal; an Immortal)

Most anciently treated of all Situations is this struggle. Into its Babel of dramatic construction all or nearly all of the others may easily enter. For this is the strife supreme; it is also the supreme folly and the supreme imprudence. It offers the most unprecedented aims of ambitions, audacious enterprises, titanesque conspiracies, Ixionian abductions; the most fascinating of enigmas; the Ideal here undergoes a rare assault of passions; prodigious rivalries develop. As for the surrounding witnesses, does not their sympathy often go to him whom they should hate? — learning of his crime, is it not sometimes their duty to punish him themselves, to sacrifice him to their faith, or to sacrifice themselves for him? Between the dearest of kindred, hatreds will break forth. Then comes the storm of disaster, the vanquished one bound to misfortune, crushed before those whom he loves, unless, — acme of horror — he has, in a transport of blind delirium, dishonored or massacred them unknowingly. Suppliants, seeking the lost loved one, advance sad theories and endeavor to disarm rancor, — but the divine vengeance has been unchained!

This remarkable grouping has been in our day almost entirely ignored. Byronists as we still are, "bon gré mal gré," we might yet dream of this superb onslaught on the heavens. But no! — we treat even the evangelical subject of the Passion, while we pass by, like owls in broad daylight, this genuinely dramatic situation, and content ourselves with sanctimoniously intoning the idyllo-didactic phrases which preceded the sacred tragedy, — itself left unseen.

A (1) — **Struggle Against a Deity:** — "The Ædonians" and "The Bassarides," "Pentheus" and "The Wool-Carders" by Aeschylus; "The Bacchantes" of Euripides; the "Christ Suffering" of Saint Gregory Nazianzen. Epic: the sixth Homeric hymn (to Dionysos); the dream of Jacob.

(2) — **Strife with the Believers in a God:** — "The Exodus of the Hebrews" by Ezekiel; "L'Empereur Julien" (Miracle of Notre-Dame, XIV Century); "Athalie." Historic instances: various persecutions. Epic: "Les Martyrs."

B (1) — **Controversy with a Deity:** — "The Book of Job." I cannot give, it is true, the date nor the place of the "premier" of "Job." But the fact of actual representation by Messieurs A, B and C and Misses X, Y and Z is no more an indispensable condition to the existence of true drama than it is an all-sufficient one. We may hold that the "premier" was given in that great Theatre of which Brahmanic legend tells; a Theatre inaugurated long before that of man, and thanks to which the gods may occupy the leisures of their eternity.

(2) — **Punishment for Contempt of a God:** — "Tchitra Yadjgna" by Vedyantha Vatchespati; "Le Festin de Pierre" (meaning the real action, which from the beginning leads toward the dénouement).

(3) — **Punishment for Pride Before a God:** — Aeschylus' "Ajax Locrian" (according to one hypothesis); Sophocles' "Thamiras;" Euripides' "Bellerophon." A Christian example: Simon the Magician.

(4) — **Presumptuous Rivalry with a God:** — "The Nurses" by Aeschylus; "Niobe" by Sophocles; "La Mère du Pape" (Miracle of Notre-Dame, XIV Century).

(5) — **Imprudent Rivalry with a Deity:** — Sophocles' "Eumele;" in part "Phaeton" by Euripides.

May it not be possible that we shall one day see treated from the point of view of this Situation, the pathetic death of Guyot-Dessaigne, Minister of Justice?

THIRTY-SECOND SITUATION

MISTAKEN JEALOUSY

(The Jealous One; the Object of Whose Possession He
is Jealous; the Supposed Accomplice; the Cause
or the Author of the Mistake)

The last element is either not personified (A), or personified in a traitor (B), who is sometimes the true rival
of the Jealous One (C).

A (1) — **The Mistake Originates in the Suspicious
Mind of the Jealous One:** — "The Worst is not Always
Certain" by Calderon; Shakespeare's "C o m e d y of
Errors;" "The Bondman" by Massinger; the "Marianne"
of Dolse and of Tristan l'Hermite; "Tancrède" and
"Marianne" by Voltaire; "la Princesse de Bagdad" by
Dumas; "Un Divorce" (Moreau, 1884); "Monna Vanna"
(Maeterlinck, 1902). How is it that Molière has not
written a comedy of jealousy upon this Situation sym-
metrical to that of L'Avare?"

(2) — **Mistaken Jealousy Aroused by a Fatal Chance:**
— Voltaire's "Zaire" and the opera of that name by de
la Nux; part of "Lucrèce Borgia." In comedy: "La
Divorcée" (Fall and Léon, 1911).

(3) — **Mistaken Jealousy of a Love Which is Purely
Platonic:** — "Love's Sacrifice" by Ford (in which the
wife is unjustly suspected). "L'Esclave du Sevoin"
(Valnay, 1881, in which it is more particularly the re-
spectful admirer who is wrongly suspected). **Of a Flirt:**
— "Suzette" (Brieux, 1908); "Four Times Seven are
Twenty-Eight" (Coolus, 1909).

(4) — Baseless Jealousy Aroused by M a l i c i o u s Rumors: — "Le Père Prodigue" by Dumas; "le Maître de Forges" (Ohnet, 1883).

B (1) — Jealousy Suggested by a Traitor Who is Moved by Hatred: — Shakespeare's "Othello" a n d "Much Ado About Nothing;" "Semiramide Riconosciuta" by Metastasio presents the fully developed dénouement of it.

(2) — The Same Case, in Which the Traitor is Moved by Self-Interest: — Shakespeare's "Cymbeline;" "La Fille du Roi d'Espagne" (Miracle of Notre-Dame, XIV Century).

(3) — The Same Case, in Which the Traitor is Moved by Jealousy and Self-Interest: — "Love and Intrigue" by Schiller.

C (1) — Reciprocal Jealousy Suggested to Husband and Wife by a Rival: — "The Portrait" by Massinger.

(2) — Jealousy Suggested to the Husband by a Dismissed Suitor: — Voltaire's "Artemire;" "Le Chevalier Jean" (Joncières, 1885).

(3) — Jealousy Suggested to the Husband by a Woman Who is in Love with Him: — "Malheur aux Pauvres" (Bouvier, 1881).

(4) — Jealousy Suggested to the Wife by a Scorned Rival: — "The Phtiotides" of Sophocles.

(5) — Jealousy Suggested to a Happy Lover by the Deceived Husband: — "Jalousie" (Vacquerie, 1888).

The number of dramatic elements brought into play already enables us to foresee many combinations for this Situation, whose improbabilities the public is always disposed to accept, however great they may be. Without abusing this indulgence, we may remark, even at first glance, that almost all the dramas above cited treat of jealousy on the part of a man, whereas experience teaches us that woman is quite as ready as man to let herself be the envious, by a rival, or by a suitor bent upon securing for himself, through the anger aroused, a pleasure otherwise out of his reach. Transference to the feminine of the cases already considered will thus furnish a series of new situations. Besides pride, self-interest, love, spite and rivalry, many other motives present themselves for the traitor or traitress; the motives mentioned may also be painted in colors yet unused. The dénouement (usually a murder, in some cases a suicide, in others a divorce) may be varied, subtilized or strengthened by secondary and instrumental characters. The same may be said for the various knots of the intrigue, for those false proofs, those diabolic suggestions from which the jealousy springs.

Under the form of "jealous spite" this situation has been used by Molière and other writers of comedy for the purpose of filling in — through the agitations it causes the principal lovers — the vacancies of the picture with minor characters.

THIRTY-THIRD SITUATION

ERRONEOUS JUDGMENT

(The Mistaken One; the Victim of the Mistake; the Cause or Author of the Mistake; the Guilty Person.)

(Any sort of mistaken judgment may here be understood, even though committed only in the thought of one person to the detriment of another.)

A (1) — False Suspicion Where Faith is Necessary: — "The Serpent Woman" by Gozzi; "L'Etudiant Pauvre" (Milloecker, 1889). One of the facets of "Henry V" is connected somewhat remotely with this situation, the incomprehension of the young prince's real character by the witnesses of his disorders. Dumas père has represented Henri de Navarre as misunderstood in the same way by his entourage.

(2) — False Suspicion (in which the jealousy is not without reason) of a Mistress: — Part of "Diane" by Augier; "Marie Stuart" by Alfieri.

(3) — False Suspicions Aroused by a Misunderstood Attitude of a Loved One: — "The Raven" by Gozzi; "Hypsipile" by Metastasio; "Theodora" (Sardou, 1884); part of "La Reine Fiammetta;" "Le Voleur" (Bernstein, 1906); "Les Grands" (Weber and Basset, 1909); "Coeur Maternel" (Franck, 1911).

(4) — By Indifference: — "Crainquebille" (France, 1909); "le Vierge" (Vallette).

B (1) — False Suspicions Drawn Upon Oneself to Save a Friend: — "Aimer Sans Savoir Qui" by Lope; "Mme. Ambros" (Widor, 1885).

(2) — **They Fall Upon the Innocent:** — "Siroès" by Metastasio; "La Grande Iza" (Bouvier, 1882); "Le Fiacre No. 13" and "Gavroche" (Dornay, 1887 and 1888); "L'Affaire des Poisons" (Sardou, 1907); "Les Pierrots" (Grillet, 1908). **Upon the Innocent Husband of the Guilty One:** — "La Criminelle" (Delacour, 1882).

(3) — **The Same Case as 2, but in Which the Innocent had a Guilty Intention:** — "Jean Cévenol" (Fraisse, 1883). **In Which the Innocent Believes Himself Guilty:** — "Le Roi de l'Argent" (Milliet, 1885); "Poupèes Electriques" (Marinetti).

(4) — **A Witness to the Crime, in the Interest of a Loved One, Lets Accusation Fall Upon the Innocent:** — "Le Secret de la Terreuse" (Busnach, 1889).

C (1) — **The Accusation is Allowed to Fall Upon an Enemy:** — "La Pieuvre" (Morel, 1885).

(2) — **The Error is Provoked by an Enemy:** — "The Palamedes" of Sophocles and of Euripides; "LeVentre de Paris" (Zola, 1887); "Le Roi Soleil" (Bernéde, 1911); "L'Homme á Deux Têtes" (Forest, 1910). This nuance alone, it will be observed, attracted the Greek tragedians, who were, so to speak, tormented by a vague conception of the Iago of a later age and who tried, in a succession of distorted types, to produce it; we seem, in these works, to be assisting at the birth of the future Devil; of the evangelic Judas — and at that of the type of Jesus in Prometheus and Dionysos. This nuance C 2 seems to me a singularly fine one; it is, for instance, that of the "anonymous letter," and it will be admitted that a more admirably repugnant gargoyle cannot be imagined than the creature who crouches with pen in claw and malignant smile, to begin such a piece of work!

(3) — **The Mistake is Directed Against the Victim by Her Brother:** (here is included, also, the Twelfth, "Hatred of Kinsmen"): — "The Brigands" by Schiller; "Don Garzia" by Alfieri.

D (1) — **False Suspicion Thrown by the Real Culprit Upon One of His Enemies:** — Corneille's "Clitandre," and "Sapho" (Gounod, 1884); "Catharine la Bâtarde" (Bell, 1881).

(2) — **Thrown by the Real Culprit Upon the Second Victim Against Whom He Has Plotted from the Beginning:** — "Le Crime d'un Autre" (Arnold and Renauld, 1908). This is pure Machiavellianism, obtaining the death of the second victim through an unjust punishment for the murder of the first. Add to this the closest relationship between the two victims and the deceived judge, and we have all these emotions assembled: discovery of the death of a relative; supposed discovery of an impious hatred between two relatives; belief even in a second case of crime, aggravated this time by a scheme of revolt; finally the duty of condemning a loved one believed to be guilty. This plot, then, is a masterly one since it groups, under the impulsion of an ambition or a vengeance, four other Situations. As for the "Machiavellianism" which has set it all in motion, it consists, for him who employs it, precisely in the method which is habitual to writers, a method here transferred to a single character; he abstracts himself, so to speak, from the drama, and, like the author, inspires in other characters the necessary feelings, unrolls before their steps the indispensable circumstances, in order that they may mechanically move toward the dénouement he desires. Thus is developed the "Artaxerce" of Metastasio.

Suppress the part of the villain, and suppose for a moment that the author has planned the dénouement desired by this traitor; the bringing about of the most cruel results from a "supposed fratricide" and the "duty of condemning a son." The author cannot otherwise combine his means to produce it. The type of the Villain (who has successively appeared in many guises) is nothing else than the author himself, masked in black, and knotting together two or three dramatic situations. He belongs, this type, to the family of the poetic Prologue, of the "Deus ex machina" (although more admissible) of the Orator of the parabases, of the Molièresque Valet, and of the Theorist (the good doctor, clergyman, journalist, "family friend"). He is in short the old Narrator of the monodramas. Nothing could be more naif, consequently, than this creature, whose unconvincing artificiality has spoiled many a scene.

(3) — False Suspicion Thrown Upon a Rival: — "Diana" (Paladilhe, 1885); "L'Ogre" (Marthold, 1890); "La Boscotte" (Mme. Maldagne, 1908).

(4) — Thrown Upon One Innocent, Because He Has Refused to be an Accomplice: — "Valentinian" by Beaumont and Fletcher; "Aetius" by Metastasio.

(5) — Thrown by a Deserted Mistress Upon a Lover Who Left Her Because He Would Not Deceive Her Husband: — "Roger-la-Honte" (Mary, 1888).

(6) — Struggle to Rehabilitate Oneself and to Avenge a Judicial Error Purposely Caused: — "La Dégringolade" (Desnard, 1881); the end of "Fiacre No. 13."

THIRTY-FOURTH SITUATION

REMORSE

(The Culprit; the Victim or the Sin; the Interrogator)

A (1) — **Remorse for an Unknown Crime:** — "Manfred" and other creations of Byron; the last of the great English dramatists, he was likewise the last adversary of Cant, which, having killed art in Spain under the name of the Inquisition, in England the first time under the name of Puritanism and in Germany under the name of Pietism, today presents itself in France, in the guise of . . . Monsieur Berenger.

(2) — **Remorse for a Parricide:** — "The Eumenides" of Aeschylus; the "Orestes" of Euripides, of Voltaire and of Alfieri; "Le Cloitre" (Verhaeren).

(3) — **Remorse for an Assassination:** — "Crime and Punishment" (Dostoievsky, 1888); "Le Coeur Révélateur" (after Poe, by Aumann, 1889). For a Judicial **Murder:** — "L'Eclaboussure" (Geraldy, 1910).

(4) — **Remorse for the Murder of Husband or Wife:** — "Thérèse Raquin" by Zola; "Pierrot, Assassin de sa Femme" (Paul Margueritte, 1888).

B (1) — **Remorse for a Fault of Love:** — "Madeleine" (Zola, 1889).

(2) — **Remorse for an Adultery:** — "Count Witold" (Rzewuski, 1889); "Le Scandale" (Bataille, 1909).

With B (1) there are connected, in one respect, the plays classed in A (1) of Situåtion XXVII.

Need I call attention to the small number, but the terrible beauty, of the above works? Is it necessary to indicate the infinite varieties of Remorse, according to: 1st, the fault committed (for this, enumerate all crimes and misdemeanors included in the legal code, plus those which do not fall under any law; the fault, moreover, may at the writer's pleasure be real or imaginary, committed without intention, or intended but not committed — which permits a "happy ending" — or both intended and committed; premeditated or not, with or without complicity, outside influences, subtlety, or what not); 2nd, the nature, more or less impressionable and nervous, of the culprit; 3rd, the surroundings, the circumstances, the morals which prepare the way for the appearance of Remorse — that figure plastic, firm and religious among the Greeks, the beneficially enervating phantasmagoria of our Middle Ages; the pious dread of a future life in recent centuries; the disturbance of the equilibrium of the social instincts and consequently of the mind according to the inferences of Zola, etc.

With Remorse is connected the Fixed Idea; through its perpetual action it recalls Madness or Criminal Passion. Often it is but "remorse for a desire," remorse the more keen in that the incessantly reviving desire nourishes it, mingles with it, and growing like a sort of moral cancer, saps the soul's vitality to the point of suicide, which is itself but the most desperate of duels. "Rene," "Werther," the maniac of the "Coeur Révélateur" and of "Bérênice" (I refer to that of Edgar Poe), and especially Ibsen's "Rosmersholm," offer significant portraits of it.

THIRTY-FIFTH SITUATION

RECOVERY OF A LOST ONE

(The Seeker; the One Found)

This is the Situation of "The Hero and the Nymph" by Kalidasa; the second part of his "Sakuntala," and the "Later Life of Rama" by Bhavabuti; the second part also of "A Winter's Tale" and "Pericles" by Shakespeare; likewise of "Berthequine" and of "Bertha au Grand Pied" (Miracles of Notre-Dame, XIV Century); of almost all of "La Reine Aux Trois Fils," another Miracle; it is the Situation of "Thyestes in Sicyon" by Sophocles and of "Alcmeon in Corinth" by Euripides. It is the dénouement of "Père Chasselas" (Athis, 1886); "Foulards Rouges" (Dornay, 1882); "La Gardienne" (Henri de Regnier); it is the old familiar plot of the "stolen child" and of stories of foundlings; of arbitrary imprisonments, from the Man in the Iron Mask (upon whom Hugo began a drama) and "Richard Coeur-de-Lion" down to recent tales of sane persons confined as lunatics. It is the point from which bursts forth so frequently that double explosion of the principal scene: "My daughter! — My mother!"

Classes A and C of Situation XI move toward the same end.

In other cases it is the part of the child to discover his father, his kinsman, and to make himself known; thus it is in the "Enfances Roland;" in "Les Enfants du Capitaine Grant" by Jules Verne and "les Aventures de Gavroche" (Darlay and Marot, 1909).

To the invariably happy and epithalamic ending to our plays built upon this Situation, and to the fortuitous coincidences with which it has been too generously interlarded, I attribute the public's final weariness of it. For does not this Situation retain more naturalness than the Nineteenth, and how fecund has been that Nineteenth, whose charm and tempting variety is all possessed by our Thirty-Fifth!

THIRTY-SIXTH SITUATION

LOSS OF LOVED ONES

(A Kinsman Slain; a Kinsman Spectator; an Executioner)

Here all is mourning. In long funeral processions we see them pass, the heroes of this Situation; they move from the dark home to the dark church, and from there to the cemetery, returning only to weep by the hearth until they leave it on the departure of another from among them.

A (1) — **Witnessing the Slaying of Kinsmen, While Powerless to Prevent It:** — The "Niobe" and "Troilus" of Aeschylus; "Polyxena" and "The Captives" of Sophocles; a part of his "Laocoon;" "The Troades" of Euripides and of Seneca.

(2) — **Helping to Bring Misfortune Upon One's People Through Professional Secrecy:** — "Les Bâillonnés" (Mme. Terni, 1909).

B — **Divining the Death of a Loved One:** — "The Intruder" and "The Seven Princesses" by Maeterlinck, the one modern master of the Thirty-Sixth, and how powerful a one!

C — **Learning of the Death of a Kinsman or Ally:** — Part of the "Rhesus" attributed to Euripides; "Penthesilea," "Psychostase" and "The Death of Achilles" by Aeschylus; "The Ethiopians" of Sophocles. Here is added the difficult rôle of the messenger of misfortune — he who bends beneath the imprecations of Cleopatra, in

Shakespeare. From comedy: — "Cent Lignes Emues" by Torquet.

D — **Relapse into Primitive Baseness, through Despair on Learning of the Death of a Loved One:** — "La Fille Sauvage" (Curel, 1902).

But embody, in a human figure, the wrong, the murder, which is abstract in most of these examples. Still bound by his helplessness, how the unfortunate who is made a spectator of the agony will struggle, appeal, and vainly implore the heavens — the Victim, meantime, humbly beseeching him who thus looks on in despair, as though he had power to save. The haughty sardonic silhouette of the Executioner dominates the scene, intensifying the keenness of the grief by his cynical pleasure in it. . . . Dante has conceived of no sharper sorrow in the circles of his Inferno.

CONCLUSION

To obtain the nuances of the Thirty-Six Situations, I have had recourse almost constantly to the same method of procedure; for example, I would enumerate the ties of friendship or kinship possible between the characters; I would determine also their degree of consciousness, of free-will and knowledge of the real end toward which they were moving. And we have seen that when it is desired to alter the normal degree of discernment in one of the two adversaries, the introduction of a second character is necessary, the first becoming the blind instrument of the second, who is at the same time invested with a Machiavellian subtlety, to such an extent does his part in the action become purely intellectual. Thus, clear perception being in the one case excessively diminished, it is, in the other, proportionately increased. Another element for modifying all the situations is the energy of the acts which must result from them. Murder, for instance, may be reduced to a wound, a blow, an attempt, an outrage, an intimidation, a threat, a too-hasty word, an intention not carried out, a temptation, a thought, a wish, an injustice, a destruction of a cherished object, a refusal, a want of pity, an abandonment, a falsehood. If the author so desires, this blow (murder or its diminutives) may be aimed, not at the object of hatred in person, but at one dear to him. Finally, the murder may be multiple and aggravated by circumstances which the law has foreseen. A third method of varying the situations: for this or that one of the two adversaries whose struggle constitutes our drama, there may be substituted a group of characters animated by a single desire, each member of the group reflecting that desire under a different light. There is, moreover (as I have already shown), no Situation which may not be combined with any one of its neighbors, nay, with two, three, four, five, six of them and more! Now, these combinations may be of many sorts; in the first case, the situations develop successively and logically one from another; in the second case they dispose themselves in a dilemma, in the midst of which hesitates the distracted hero; in the third case, each one of them will appertain to a particular group or a particular rôle; in the fourth, fifth, sixth cases, etc., they are represented according to two, or according to all three of the cases already brought together in one situation, and together they escape from it, but the majority of them fall therefrom into a position not less critical, which may even offer but a choice between two courses equally painful; after finding a way between this Scylla and Charybdis, the very leap by which they escape precipitates them into a final Situation resulting from the preceding ones, and which sweeps them all away together. . . . This, be it understood, is but one combination among a thousand, for I cannot here elaborate the system by which this study of the Thirty-Six Situations may be continued, and by means of which they may be endlessly multiplied; that is a subject for a separate work upon the "Laws of Literary Invention."

The composition or arrangement of the chosen Situations — and at the same time of the episodes and characters introduced — may be deduced in a manner somewhat novel and interesting, from the same theory of the "Thirty-Six." Considering, in effect, that "every dramatic situation springs from a conflict between two principal directions of effort" (whence at the same time comes our dread of the victor and our pity for the vanquished), we shall have to choose, at the rising of the

curtain, between two beginnings; we must decide which
of the two adversaries pre-exists. This leads us infal-
libly to make of the second the cause (innocent or re-
sponsible) of the drama, since it is his appearance which
will be the signal for the struggle. The first, who especially enlists our attention, is the Protagonist, already
present in the earliest Thespian tragedy, altogether lyric,
descriptive and analytic; the second — the obstacle aris-
ing or supervening — is the Antagonist, that principle
of the action which we owe to the objective and Homeric
genius of Aeschylus. One of two strongly opposing
colors will thus dominate the entire work, according as
we shall choose, near the beginning, which of the two
parties shall possess the greater power, the greater
chance of victory.

Aristotle has taught us to distinguish between "simple" tragedy (in which the superiority remains upon the
same side until the end, and in which, consequently,
there is no sudden change of fortune, no surprise) and
"complex" tragedy (the tragedy of surprise, of vicissitude), wherein this superiority passes from one camp to
the other. Our dramatists have since refined upon the
latter; in those of their pieces which are least complicated, they double the change of fortune, thus leading
ingeniously to the return of the opposed powers, at the
moment of the spectator's departure, to the exact posi-
tions which they occupied when he entered the hall; in
their plays of complicated plot, they triple, quadruple,
quintuple the surprise, so long as their imaginations and
the patience of the public will permit. We thus see, in
these vicissitudes of struggle, the first means of varying
a subject. It will not go very far, however, since we
cannot, however great our simplicity, receive from the
drama, or from life, more than one thousand three hundred and thirty-two surprises. — One thousand three
hundred and thirty-two? Obviously; what is any keen
surprise if not the passing from a state of calm into a
Dramatic Situation, or from one Situation into another,
or again into a state of calm? Perform the multiplication; result, one thousand, three hundred and thirty-two.

Shall we now inquire whence arise these vicissitudes, these unexpected displacements of equilibrium? Clearly in some influence, proceeding from a material object, a circumstance, or a third personage. Upon this Third Actor — whose introduction into the drama was the triumph of Sophocles — must rest what is called the Plot. He is the unforeseen element, the ideal striven for by the two parties and the surrounding characters; he is fantastically divided and multiplied, by two, by three, by ten, by even more, to the point of encumbering the scene; but he is always himself, always easily recognizable. Some of his fragments become "Instruments," some, "Disputed Objects," some, "Impelling Forces;" they range themselves sometimes beside the Protagonist, sometimes near the Antagonist, or, moving here and there, they provoke that downfall the incessant avoidance of which is called — for events as for mankind — Progress. In this way they clearly show their origin — that "Role-Lien" (Jocaste in "Seven Against Thebes," Sabine in "Horace") under which the Third Actor was germinating in Aeschylean tragedy, without yet taking a positive part in the action.

It will be seen that the appearance of these figures of the second plan, these Choruses, Confidants, Crowds, Clowns, even Figurants re-enforced by those of the o r i g i n a l groundwork, precursors whose importance ranges from Tiresias to the Messenger of "Oedipus the King," from prophet to porter, modifies most powerfully the effect of the ensemble, especially if we reflect that each one of these, considered separately, has his own especial motives for action, motives soon apparent in regard to the characters who surround him, in some dramatic situation subordinate to the dominant one, but none the less real; the turns and changes of the general action will affect him in some particular way, and the consequences, to him, of each vicissitude, of each effort, of each act and dénouement, contribute to the spectator's final impression. If the Third Actor, for instance, be a Disputed Object, it becomes necessary to take into account his first and his last possessor, the diverse relations which he has successively had with them, and his own preferences. If he appear as Inspirer or Instigator, we must consider (aside from his degree of consciousness or unconsciousness, of frankness or dissimulation, and of Will proper) the perseverance which he brings to his undertaking; if he be unconscious, the discovery which he may make of his own unconsciousness; if he be a deceiver, the discoveries which others may make of his dissimulation ("others" here meaning perhaps a single character, perhaps the spectator). These remarks also apply to the "Instrumental" rôle; and not alone these remarks, but those also which concern the "Object," are applicable to the Role-Lien.

I have already observed that this last rôle, and the triple hypostasis of the Third Actor, may be reproduced in numerous exemplars within one play. On the other hand, two, three, or all four of them may be fused in a single figure (Lien-Instrumental, Object-Instigator, Instrument-Lien-Object, etc.), combinations which present themselves, like the combinations of the Situations, already considered, in varied array. Sometimes the hero who unites in himself these divers rôles plays them simultaneously — perhaps all of them toward an individual or group, perhaps one or several of them toward an individual or group, and another rôle wherein these rôles mingle, toward some other individual or group; sometimes these various rôles will be successively played toward the same individual or group, or toward several; sometimes, finally, the hero plays these rôles now simultaneously, and again successively.

But it is not possible to detail in these pages, even if I so desired, the second part of the Art of Combination; that which we in France call by the somewhat feeble term (as Goethe remarked) "composition." All that I have here undertaken to show is, first, that a single study must create, at the same time, the episodes or actions of the characters, and the characters themselves: for upon the stage, what the latter are may be known only by what they do; next, how invention and composition, those two modes of the Art of Combination (not Imagination, empty word!) will, in our works to come, spring easily and naturally from the theory of the Thirty-Six Situations.

Thus, from the first edition of this little book, I might offer (speaking not ironically but seriously) to dramatic authors and theatrical managers, ten thousand scenarios, totally different from those used repeatedly upon our stage in the last fifty years * * * * * * "The scenarios will be, needless to say, of a realistic and effective character. I will contract to deliver a thousand in eight days. For the production of a single gross, but twenty-four hours are required. Prices quoted on single dozens. Write or call, No. 19, Passage de l'Elysee des Beaux-Arts. The Situations will be detailed act by act, and, if desired, scene by scene" * * *

But I hear myself accused, with much violence, of an intent to "kill imagination." "Enemy of fancy!" "Destroyer of wonders!" "Assassin of prodigy!" * * * These and similar titles cause me not a blush.

A singular history, in truth, is that of the "Imagination." Certainly no one in classic times thought of priding himself upon it. Far from it! Every novelty on its first appearance, hastened to support itself by appeal to some antique authority. From 1830 dates the accession to the literary throne of this charlatanesque "faculty," analysis of which is, it would seem, eternally interdicted. The results of this new régime were not slow in appearing, and they may be seen, in their final decay, among the last successors of ultra-romantic Romanticism. Mysterious crime, judicial error, followed by the inevitable love affair between the children of slayer and victim; a pure and delicate working-girl in her tiny room, a handsome young engineer who passes by; a kind-hearted criminal, two police spies, the episode of the stolen child; and in conclusion, for the satisfaction of sentimental souls, a double love-match at the very least, and a suicide imposed upon the villain — this, one year with another, is the product of the Imagination. For the rest, in the whole field of dramatic romanticism (which cor-

responds so well to the Carrache school of painting)
Hugo alone has created, thanks to what? — to a technical process patiently applied to the smallest details, —
the antithesis of Being and of Seeming.

One vigorous blow was, for the moment, given to
this legend of the Imagination by Positivism, which as-
serted that this so-called creative faculty was merely the
kaleidoscope of our memories, stirred by chance. But it
did not sufficiently insist upon the inevitably banal and
monotonous results of these chance stirrings, some of
our memories — precisely those least interesting and
least personal — repeating themselves a thousand times
in our minds, returning mercilessly in all manner of
methodless combinations. These souvenirs of innumerable readings of the products of imitation in our neo-
classic and Romantic past, envelop and overwhelm us
unless we turn to that observation of nature which was
pointed out by the Naturalists' initiative as an element
of renovation. Even the Naturalists themselves have
too often viewed reality athwart their bookish recollec-
tions; they have estimated too highly the power of the
artistic temperament, however vigorous it may be, in as-
suming that it could interpose itself, alone and stripped
of all convention, by a simple effort of will, between Nature and the literary product to be engendered. Thus
"La Bête Humaine" has repeated the "judicial error" in
that special form which is as common in books as it is
rare in life; thus the starting-point of "L'Œuvre" is
merely the converse of the "thesis" of the Goncourts,
and Daudet; thus reminiscences of "Madame Bovary"
appear in many a study of similar cases, which should,
nevertheless, remain quite distinct; — and thus has appeared, in the second generation of "naturalists," a new
school of imitators and traditionalists.

And all the old marionettes have reappeared, inflated
with philosophic and poetic amplifications, but too often
empty of symbolism, as of naturalism and humanism.

As to the methods of the Art of Combining, the truth
may be grasped by one bold look, one triumphant glance

at all these phantoms of trite thought, as they stand in their respective places in the foregoing categories. Any writer may have here a starting-point for observation and creation, outside the world of paper and print, a starting-point personal to himself, original in short, — which does not in the least mean improbable or unconvincing, since many situations which have today an appearance of improbability have merely been disfigured by persons who, not knowing how to create new ones, have complicated the old, entangling themselves in their own threads.

Especially will the invention of an unusual story, the discovery of a "virgin field" (to use the naturalists' term), be made so easy as to be almost valueless. We are not unaware of the importance, in the perfecting of Greek art, of the fact that it was circumscribed and restricted to a small number of legends (Œdipus, Agamemnon, Phaedra, etc.), which each poet had in his turn to treat, thus being unable to escape comparison, step by step, with each of his predecessors, so that even the least critical of spectators could see what part his personality and taste had in the new work. The worst which may be said of this tradition is that it rendered originality more difficult. By a study of the Thirty-Six Situations and their results, the same advantage may be obtained without its accompanying inconvenience. Thenceforth Proportion alone will assume significance.

By proportion I mean, not a collection of measured formulæ which evoke familiar memories, — but the bringing into battle, under command of the writer, of the infinite army of possible combinations, ranged according to their probabilities. Thus, to make manifest the truth or the impression which, until now, has been perceptible to him alone, the author will have to overlook in a rapid view the field before him, and to choose such of the situations and such of the details as are most appropriate to his purpose. This method — or, if you will, this freedom and this power — he will use, not only in the choice, the limitation and fertilization of his subject, but in his observation and meditation. And he will no more run the risk of falsifying, through pre-conceived ideas, the vision of reality than does the painter, for example, in his application of laws equally general, and likewise controlled by constant experimentation, — the divine laws of perspective!

Proportion, finally realizable in the calm bestowed by complete possession of the art of combining, and recovering the supreme power long ago usurped by "good taste" and by "imagination," will bring about the recognition of that quality more or less forgotten in modern art, — "beauty." By this I mean, not the skillful selection of material from nature, but the skillful and exact representation — with no groping, no uncertainty, no retention of superfluities — of the particular bit of nature under observation.

But it is more than this, for these two definitions, the eclectic and the naturalist, concern but a limited number of the arts, and but one side of them; that small number to which imitation is open (painting, literature of character, and, in a limited way, sculpture), and that side of them which is purely imitative. What significance have these two definitions (both of which rest upon the reproduction of reality, the one exalting and the other belittling it) if they be confronted with Music, with the didactic poetry of a Hesiod, with the Vedic incantations, with true statuary, simplified and significant, from the mighty chisel-strokes of Phidias or of the XIII Century, with purely ornamental or decorative art, — the "beauty" of a demonstration in geometry, — or finally with Architecture, now reviving in silence and obscurity, that art which comes periodically to reunite and, like an ark, to rescue the others, that art which shall once more return to lead us away from the prematurely senile follies of our delettanti and sectarians.

Upon a like height stands a principle greater than Naturalism with its experimental method, or Idealism which gives battle to it, — Logic.

It is by methods of logic that Viollet-le-Duc has enabled us to estimate truly the marvels of our "grand siècle," the XIII Century, substituting (to cite only this) for the simple admiration of 1830 before each stone saint so "picturesquely" perched upon the point of an ogive, the builders' explanation: that a stone of the exact weight and dimensions of the saint was there absolutely necessary, to prevent the breaking of the ogive under a double lateral pressure, — whence the instinctive satisfaction it gives our eyes. It is a great misfortune that the understanding of that magnificent age in which a Saint Louis presided over the multiple communal life, an age whose only equal in the world's history is that in which Pericles directed, from the Athenian metropolis, an identical movement, — that this understanding, which would be so useful to us, should have been horribly compromised in the Romantic carnival. Hugo's "Notre-Dame de Paris," wherein the public believed it beheld a portrait of our "Moyen-âge" (a most absurd appellation, by the way), represents it, by a singular choice, as already long dead, — after the Hundred Years' War which bled us to the point where we fell, passive and defenseless, under the domination of the Florentine national art called "renaissant," and then of various other influences, ancient and foreign, during four centuries. And, down to the very moment at which I write, the literary productions upon the subject of this most incomparable period of our past have been but pitiable affairs. But yesterday, a Renan was writing of ogival art as an effort which had been impotent ("Souvenirs d'Enfance et de Jeunesse") or which at most had fathered works of no enduring character ("Prière sur l'Acrople"); the very Catholic Huysmans, in his "En Route," was making the most astounding salad of Roman vaulting, Primitive painting, Gregorian plain-chant, — a salad whose recipe is "the Faith" and which is called, naturally, the "Moyen-âge," — that age which embraces ten centuries of humanity, plus one-third of humanity's authentic history, three epochs strongly antagonistic to each other, peoples widely diverse and opposed; a something equivalent to a marriage between Alcibiades and Saint Genevieve.

The "Moyen-âge," or, to speak more accurately, the

XII, XIII, and XIV Centuries, were not in the least
fantastic and freakish; this is the character merely of
an occasional generation, such as that of Louis-Philippe.
Neither were they mystic, in the present sense of that
word. The architecture of those centuries grew, stone
by stone, plan by plan, out of the most practical of reasons. In their sculpture there was nothing "naive" —
the naivete is ours, when we so estimate that sculpture,
which is far more realistic than our own; and if, persist-
ing in the contrary opinion, we cling to the weird forms
of the gargoyles, it may be said that, born of a symbolism akin to those of Egypt and Greece, they represent
analogies equally ingenious and profound. In this period arose Thomism, lately called back into a position
of honor to combat Positivism, and which realized so
happy a harmony between Aristotelianism and Christian
faith, between science and theology. In this period, too,
were born the natural sciences, and, in the minds of its
poets, evolved the laws by which our poetry lives today,
those rhythms which through Ronsard we still hear, that
Rhyme which we gave to all Europe, — and, at the same
time, thy groined vaultings, O little town of Saint-Denis,
suzerain oriflamme, pilot-barque of France! All these
were born, and grew, beneath the grave gaze of the same
wisdom which, on the Ionian shores, was called Athene.

Toward a new aspect of the same logic our own age
already turns, since, having drunk of that antiquity by
whose forces we ruled Europe a second time in the
XVII Century; having drunk of the latest of great foreign influences, the Germanic, we are returning to reality
and to the future. Thus, when each Greek city had absorbed the neighboring local cults (its "foreign influences") and the Oriental cults (the "antiquity" of that
day), the most beautiful of mythologies were formed.
It is, at least, toward an art purely logical, purely technical, and of infinitely varied creations, that all our literary tendencies seem to me to be converging. In that
direction proceed Flaubert and Zola, those rugged pio-
neers, Ibsen, Strindberg, and all writers deliberately un-
mindful of their libraries, as the Hellenes were of bar-

barian literature; there moves Maeterlinck, having reduced action to the development of a single idea;
Verlaine, delivering from conventional rules t r u e
rhythm, which makes for itself its own rules; Mallarmé,
prince of ellipse, clarifying syntax and expelling clouds
of our little parasite words and tattered formulæ; in that
direction Moréas calls us, but without freeing himself,
unfortunately, from the Italianism of our so-called Re-
naissance; all these, and others not less glorious, a whole
new generation springing up, futurists, "loups," cubists,
seem to me to be seeking the same goal, the final aboli-
tion of all absolute authority, even that of Nature and
of our sciences her interpreters; and the erection upon
its débris of simple logic, of an art solely technical, and
thus capable of revealing an unknown system of harmony; in brief, an artists' art.

In literature, in dramatic literature which is the special subject of our consideration, the investigation of
Proportion of which I have above spoken will show us
the various "general methods" of presenting any situation whatever. Each one of these "general methods,"
containing a sort of canon applicable to all situations,
will constitute for us an "order" analogous to the orders
of architecture, and which, like them, will take its place
with other orders, in a dramatic "system." But the systems, in their turn, will come together under certain
rubrics yet more general, comparisons of which will furnish us many a subject for reflection. In that which we
might call Enchantment, there meet, oddly enough, systems as far apart in origin as Indian drama; certain
comedies of Shakespeare ("A Midsummer Night's
Dream;" "The Tempest"), the "fiabesque" genre of
Gozzi, and "Faust;" the Mystery brings together the
works of Persia, Thespis and the pre-Aeschyleans, "Prometheus," the book of "Job," the stage of the tragic
Ezekiel, of Saint Gregory Nazianzen, of Hroswitha, the
Jeux and Miracles of our XIII Century, the Autos; here,
Greek tragedy and the psychologists' imitations of it;
there, English, German and French drama of 1830; still
nearer, the type of piece which from the background of

China, through Lope and Calderon, Diderot and Goethe, has come to cover our stage today. . . .

It will be remembered that, when we were cataloguing dramatic production in its thirty-six classes, an assiduous effort to establish, for every exceptional case found in one of them, symmetrical cases in the other thirty-five caused unforeseen subjects to spring up under our very feet. Likewise, when we shall have analyzed these orders, systems and groups of systems, when we shall have measured with precision their resemblances and their differences, and classified them, or, one by one, according to the questions considered, shall have brought them together or separated them, — we shall necessarily remark that numerous combinations have been forgotten. Among these the New Art will choose.

Would that I might be able to place the first, the obscurest foundation-stone of its gigantic citadel! There, drawing about her the souls of the poets, the Muse shall rise before this audience re-assembled from ancient temples, before these peoples who gathered of yore around Herodotus and Pindar; she will speak the new language — the Dramatic — a language too lofty for the comprehension of the single soul, however great it be, — a language not of words but of thrills, such as that spoken to armies, — a language in truth addressed to thee, O Bacchus, dispenser of glory, soul of crowds, delirium of races, abstract, but One and Eternal! Not in one of our parlor-like pasteboard reductions of the Roman demicircus will this come to pass, but upon a sort of mountain, flooded with light and air, — raised, thanks to our conquest of iron added to the constructive experience of the Middle Ages; offered to the nation by those who have still held to the vanity of riches, — a greater thing than the theatre of Dionysos where gathered thirty thousand people, greater than that of Ephesus wherein sat, joyous, a hundred and fifty thousand spectators, an immense orifice-like crater in which the earth seems to encompass the very heavens.

ALPHABETICAL INDEX

Of the Plays, Novels, Etc., Classified in the Situations of this Work

A

E

Edith, by Bois	V	C	
Egmont, by Goethe	V	C	
1812, by Nigond	XIV	A	1
Electra, by Sophocles	IV	A	1
" by Euripides	IV	A	1
" by Attilius	IV	A	1
" by Q. Cicero	IV	A	1
" by Pradon	IV	A	1
" by Longepierre	IV	A	1
" by Crébillon	IV	A	1
" by Rochefort	IV	A	1
" by Chénier	IV	A	1
" by Guillard	IV	A	1
Eleusinians, by Aeschylus	IV	A	2
Emigrants (Les), by Hirsch	XV	A	1
Emigré (L'), by Bourget	XXVIII	A	1
Emilia Galotti, by Lessing	XXIV	C	
Empereur Julien (L') Miracle of Notre-Dame	XXXI	A	2
Enchantement (L'), by Bataille	XIV	A	4
En détresse, by Fèvre	VII	C	2
Enemy of the People (An), by Ibsen	V	C	
Enigma (The), by Hervieu	XXV	D	1
Enfant du Temple (L'), by de Polhes	XX	A	4
Enfants du Capitaine Grant (Les), by Verne	XXXV		
Enfants naturels (Les), by Sue	XVIII	A	2
En grève, by Hirsch	XXIV	A	7
Eole, by Euripides	XXVI	C	2
Epigones (The), by Aeschylus	III	A	1
Epigones (The), by Sophocles	IV	A	1
Erechtheus, by Euripides	XXIII	A	1
Eriphyle, by Sophocles	IV	A	1
Eriphyle, by Voltaire	IV	A	1
Esclarmonde, by Massenet	XVII	B	2
Esclave du devoir (L'), by Valnay	XXXII	A	3
Esméralda (La), by Hugo	XXIV	A	11
Esther, by Racine	I	C	1
Etau (L'), by A. Sardou	XVI	D	
Ethiopians (The), by Sophocles	XXXVI	C	
Et ma soeur?, by Rabier	XXVIII	B	
Etrangère (L'), by Dumas fils	III	B	7
Etudiant pauvre (L'), by Milloecker	XXXIII	A	1
Etudiants russes, by Gilkin	XXVII	D	1
Eumele, by Sophocles	XVII	A	1
Eumenides (The), by Aeschylus	and XXXI	B	5
	XXXIV	A	2
	and I	A	1
Europa, by Aeschylus	X	A	
Euryale, by Sophocles	XIX	B	2
Eurysaces, by Sophocles	I	C	2
Evangéliste (L'), by Daudet	XX	B	1

H

ALPHABETICAL INDEX OF AUTHORS

A

B

E

F

K

L

Massinger: The Bondman	XXXII	A	1
" The Portrait	XXXII	C	1
Mathey: Zoe Chien-Chien	IV	A	2
Maujan: Jacques Bonhomme	VIII	B	1
Maupassant: Pierre et Jean	XIV	A	1
Mazel: Les Amazones	XXIX	A	4
Meilhac: La Veuve joyeuse	XXVIII	A	2
Melitus: Œdipus	XVIII	A	1
Mendès: Glatigny	XXIV	A	9
" Les Mères ennemies	XXV	B	2
" La Reine Fiammette	XXIX	B	3
	and XXXIII	A	3
Mercereau: Mon frère	XIII	A	2
Merimee: Colomba	III	A	1
Messager: Francois les bas-bleus	XXIV	B	6
Metastasio: Cato	V	C	
	and XXIX	A	2
" Alexander	V	C	
" The Desert Isle	XII	B	
" Cyrus	XIII	C	
	and XIX	B	3
" Antigone	XIV	B	1
" Demophon	XIX	A	1
" Olympiade	XIX	B	1
" Regulus	XX	A	1
" Themistocles	XX	A	2
" Dido	XX	B	3
" Achilles in Scyros	XX	B	3
" Hypsip le	XXIII	B	2
" Hylermnestre	XXIII	B	3
" Demetrius	XXIV	A	5
" Semiramide riconosciuta	XXIV	B	8
	and XXXII	B	1
" Adrien	XXIV	C	
" Zenobia	XXV	C	2
" Nitetis	XXVIII	A	1
" The Chinese Hero	XXVIII	A	1
" The Shepherd King	XXVIII	C	1
" Siroes	XXXIII	B	2
" Artaxerxes	XXXIII	D	2
" Ætius	XXXIII	D	4
Méténier: La Casserole	III	A	7
Michaud d'Humiac: Le Cœur de Se-hor	XXVII	D	6
Mikhael: Le Cor fleuri	XXIV	B	3
Milliet: Le Roi de l'argent	XXXIII	B	3
Milloecker: L'Etudiant pauvre	XXXIII	A	1
Miral: Lydie	XXIX	A	4
Mirbeau: Les Affaires sont les affaires	XXVII	A	3
Moses (?): Job	XXX	B	1
Molière: Don Juan	V	B	
Montépin: La Policière	XXVII	C	

N

O

P

Sardou: Fedora	XXIX	B	5
" Theodora	XXXIII	A	2
" L'Affaire des Poissons	XXXIII	B	2
Sardou (André): L'Etau	XVI	D	
Schiller: William Tell	III	B	6
	and VIII	B	2
Schiller: The Brigands	V	A	
	and XXXIII	C	3
" Fiesco	VIII	A	1
" Don Carlos	XIV	B	3
	and XXVI	B	2
" The Bride of Messina	XVIII	A	2
" Marie Stuart	XXIV	B	2
" Wallenstein	XXX	A	3
" Love and Intrigue	XXXII	B	3
Second: La Viscomtesse Alice	V	D	
Sedaine: Richard Cœur-de-Lion	X	D	1
	and XXXV		
See: L'Indiscret	XVII	A	1
Seneca: The Phœnissæ	XIII	A	1
" Thyestes	XIII	A	2
" Octavia	XV	B	
" Hercules Furens	XVI	A	1
" Œdipus	XVIII	A	1
" Medea	XXV	A	1
" Hercules on Œta	XXV	B	1
" Hippolyte	XXVI	B	1
" The Trojan Women	XXXVI	A	1
Séverine: Sainte-Hélene	III	A	2
Shakespeare: King John	I	A	1
" The Tempest	III	B	1
" The Merchant of Venice	III	B	6
	and XI	B	2
" Hamlet	IV	A	1
	and XIII	C	
" Troilus and Cressida	V	C	
" Richard II	VI	B	
" Timon of Athens	VI	C	1
" Coriolanus	VI	C	1
	and XII	B	
" King Lear	VI	C	1
" Henry VI	VI	B	
" Henry V	IX	B	1
	and XXXIII	A	1
" Pericles	XXXV		
	and XI	B	2
" Two Gentlemen of Verona	XIV	D	
" Measure for Measure	XXI	D	2
" Antony and Cleopatra	XXII	A	4
" Henry VIII	XXV	B	5
" Romeo and Juliet	XXIX	B	6

Sophocles:	Hermione	X	C 2
"	Polyidus	XI	A
"	Women of Scyros	XI	C 2
"	Ulysses	XI	C 3
"	Philoctetes	XII	A
"	Helen Reclaimed	XII	C
"	Thyestes II	XIII	A 2
"	Ajax	XVI	B
"	Eumele	XVII	A 1
"	Pelias	XVII	C 4
		and XIX	E
"	Œdipus the King	XVIII	A 1
"	Creusa	XIX	B 1
"	Telephus	XIX	B 1
"	Euryale	XIX	B 2
"	Alexander	XIX	C 1
"	Procris	XIX	G 1
"	Amphitryon	XIX	F 3
"	Alceste	XXI	A 1
"	Iphigenia	XXIII	A 1
"	Iobate	XXVI	B 1
"	Lemnian Women	XXIII	B 2
"	Women of Colchis	XXV	A 1
"	Antigone	XX	A 3
"	The Maidens of Trachis	XXV	B 1
"	Alcmeon	XXV	B 4
"	Phædra	XXVI	B 1
"	Thamiras	XXXI	B 3
"	Niobe	XXXI	B 4
"	Eumele	XXXI	B 5
"	The Phtiotides	XXXII	C 4
"	Palamede	XXXIII	C 2
"	Thyestes at Sicyon	XXXV	
"	The Captives	XXXVI	A 1
"	Laocoon	XXXVI	A 1
"	Polyxena	XXXVI	A 1
"	The Ethiopians	XXXVI	C
Soubhata:	The Message of Angada	X	C 2
Soudraka:	The Earthen Toy-cart	XXIV	A 5
Soundara Misra:	Abhirama mani	X	C 2
Speroni:	Canace	XXVI	C 2
Spontini:	The Danaides	XXIII	B 3
Stace:	Agave	XXXI	A 1
Stein:	La Veuve joyeuse	XXVIII	A 2
Sue:	Les Enfants naturels	XVIII	A 2

T

Tarbé:	Monsieur de Morat	XXV	B 3
Tasso:	Torrismond	XVIII	A 2
"	Jerusalem Delivered	XIX	G 1

ANONYMOUS